MW00344826

EVERYONE HAS A
STORY

———— ◆ ————

PAUL THOMAS
JORDAN

HELEN JORDAN DAVIS, Ph.D., Th.D.

Everyone Has A Story: Paul Thomas Jordan

by Helen Jordan Davis, Ph.D., Th.D.

Copyright 2015 by Helen Jordan Davis, Ph.D., Th.D.

All rights reserved.

ISBN: 978-0-9961897-0-5

Published by: Principle Books Publishers

This book and parts thereof may not be reproduced in any form, stored in a retrieval system or transmitted in any form by any means (electronic, mechanical, photocopy, recording or otherwise) without prior written permission of the author, except as provided by United States of America copyright law.

Scripture taken from the King James Version. Used by permission. All rights reserved.

Cover by Tina Schinneller of Image Media Resource.

Ebook ISBN: 978-0-9961897-1-2

First printing: June 2015

Book available at amazon.com. Ebook available on amazon.com, kobobooks.com, and the ibooks store

Dedication

I don't know that this will be my last writing, but I want to write it as if it will be.

Thinking about the articles I wrote forty-five years ago, there is still agreement between the young Paul I was then and the old Paul I am now. I still believe the Golden Rule should always be followed: Treat others the way you would want to be treated.

Did I ever do anything as a policeman that I regret? One thing has bothered me for forty-five years: a friend ran a stop sign, and I gave him a ticket, charged him $15, when I could have given him a break. When I see him, he's always friendly and has never said a word against me. Forty-five years later, I think about him and the incident. We can't go back and do over, or I would.

On the other hand, a man I charged with DUI pleaded with me to reduce the charge to Reckless Driving. He asked again and again, and I finally did as he asked. That man still thanks me almost every time I see him. His life has changed for the better, and I've never been sorry I reduced the charge.

I guess we can't go through life without some regrets. I know I've made plenty of mistakes in my 75 years, and I'm so glad Jesus said that if we'd just confess our sins, He would forgive. We all fall short; there's none righteous but Jesus Himself.

What are my concerns today? Well, I see our country just about turning its back on Israel. I sure hope that will never happen. Then we still have somewhat of a race problem, it seems. I was working with a very close friend some time back when we were discussing the fact that, he as a black man and I as a white one, neither had any control over or choice in the color of our skin. The difference in our skin color doesn't make any difference in our friendship. I think the world of him and his family. We're Christian brothers; he's a Deacon in his church, and I am in mine.

I would like to dedicate this book to him, Robert Watson, Jr., and several others.

Bobby Looney was my closest friend growing up. He, Preston Vickery, and I called ourselves "The Three Stooges." Preston recently went on to heaven ahead of us. I have always valued their friendship.

Then there's Jerry Smith, a man I work with, who is like a big brother to me. He has a wonderful life story that my sister will soon be writing, too, so look for his book.

All of these have greatly enriched my life, and I'll always be grateful.

As I close, I just want to say: "May God bless each one who reads this book, and please remember that the Bible is the MAIN book. Please read it, too."

Paul Thomas Jordan

Table of Contents

Foreword 6

Preface 7

Introduction 8

Chapter One: His Town, Anderson 10

Chapter Two: Childhood 13

Chapter Three: Teen Years 29

Chapter Four: Adulthood 35

Chapter Five: Policeman 38

Chapter Six: Newspaper Column 53

Chapter Seven: New Career 126

Chapter Eight: Today 139

Endnotes 142

Other Books by Helen Jordan Davis 143

Foreword

Great book! Really holds your attention. I couldn't wait to read what was on the next page, even though Paul is my brother, and I knew most of his story!

I love the book!

Betty Jordan McClain

I have enjoyed reading this book about my favorite man on the earth, my Dad. He has always been one of the most kind-hearted people I've ever known. He taught me to just trust in God when things don't go well, and stay close to Him by reading the Word and praying every day.

May reading these wonderful stories of his bring you as much joy as it has brought me!

Paula Jordan Garton

A wonderful story about a wonderful person! I found myself playing outside along with young Paul and the neighborhood gang, walking with him down the streets on patrol, sitting beside him as he wrote his columns, etc. His story is unique, yet it offers a point of view on subjects we still deal with in 2015.

With a quick wit and a warm heart, he brings joy wherever he goes. I'm impressed with his biblical knowledge, his memory for details, and that he is a strong advocate for what is right and fair.

I feel honored to be his grand-niece!

Lauren Pledger Lunney

Preface

A man (or woman) of 75 is a composite of what he was at all the stages of his life. His infancy, childhood, school years, adolescence, young adulthood, and middle age are the layers beneath what you see when you look at his 75 year-old face. You can't see the layers underneath because they're covered by the 75-year-old layer, but they're there just the same and need to be remembered. We should still see him as the handsome teenager, the robust 35 year-old, and the maturing 40 or 50 year-old with our mind's eye when we look in his face. We need to remember his story, especially if we have been privileged to share some of those stages with him.

I remember seeing a display at the Visitation for a church friend named Bill who had died. The display had write-ups of awards and other honors he had received. I remember thinking, "I wish I had known about that. I could have talked with him about that experience. I should have appreciated his accomplishments more." Now it was too late.

That's really the motivation for this book. I'm happy to say that I shared a childhood with this book's title character. Adulthood, though, found us living far apart, and though I saw him occasionally, I really was too involved with my own life to realize to any depth what all was going on in his. I'm proud of what he has accomplished in life, and I'm proud to say that he's my brother—and it's not too late to talk about his experiences and appreciate his accomplishments.

Here's his story.

Introduction

Beginning

He was given three Bible names, Paul, Thomas, Jordan. Born the third child of textile workers in a town of textile workers, Anderson, South Carolina, he had arrived on March 17th, 1940.

March 17th, of course, is St. Patrick's Day in honor of the wonderful Christian who evangelized Ireland and is credited with preventing an overthrow of the government there. This he did after having been kidnapped and enslaved for six years by the very people he later returned to evangelize.

Though they shared that day for recognition, Paul naturally was not on the same honor level with Patrick, but you'll see that throughout his life he, too, has had a close connection with the God of the Bible and has shared many of the same character traits with Patrick. He has loved the concept of good triumphing over evil, exactly what Patrick had accomplished.

From the cop protecting the innocent people of his city by removing from the streets those who break the law, to the cowboy or lawman in the white hat winning over the outlaw who is endangering the people of the town in the western movies he loves, the common theme is the same—always good winning over evil.

Read on.

Clyde, Paul, Betty

Chapter One
His Town, Anderson

Much of the following information on Anderson and Anderson County comes from the book *South Carolina Postcards Volume IX* by Howard Woody.

> *The first Europeans to visit Anderson County were in the Spanish explorer Hernando De Soto's expedition, passing up the east side of the Savannah River Valley through Anderson County in 1540.*[1]

This was the Cherokee territory that would one day become Anderson County, but it wouldn't become the Anderson District until 1826.

> *De Soto sought gold and asked the Cherokee Indians where it could be found and his quest led him west into Georgia. In 1757 a treaty with the Cherokee Indians opened all their lands in lower South Carolina up to the northwest area to the European settlers. ... Robert Anderson, from Virginia, surveyed this area in 1765 and then settled in the Pendleton area. General Andrew Pickens ... negotiated the Cherokee treaty of 1785. ... After the peace with the Indians, settlers including the Scots and the Scots-Irish traveled south on the Great Philadelphia Wagon Trail in covered wagons from Virginia, Maryland, and Pennsylvania. The white population in 1790 was 8,731 and increased to 17,760 in 1800.*[2]

One of Paul's ancestors, Solomon Loftis, who had a Cherokee mother and European father, was born around 1800, and is said to have walked from Virginia to Anderson County. Why he was in Virginia is unknown. No doubt the path he took was the lower portion of this well-traveled Great Philadelphia Wagon Trail.

The land was productive and small farms and larger plantations thrived with corn, cotton, grain, and tobacco crops. ... On May 1, 1865, Union troops came to the town of Anderson looking for the Confederate Treasury and its gold. Instead, they found a large stock of fine liquor in the cellar of the B.F. Crayton building and became drunk and did not burn the town.[3]

Union General Sherman did burn Atlanta and from there burned a wide swath all the way to the sea. Anderson was spared.

Cotton Mills

Near the end of the 18th century, industries related to Anderson's cotton crop began to develop where railroads came close to creeks and rivers. Cotton mills were constructed to use water power to produce fabric from the cotton of this county. The Anderson County mills processed over three-fourths of the county's cotton production in 1901. ... Anderson was the fourth wealthiest county in South Carolina in 1901.[4]

The city's first cotton mill was in production in 1890 using steam power. In 1894 Anderson's first hydro-electric power plant at High Shoals began serving the city. Anderson Cotton Mill converted to electricity and became the first electric cotton mill in the United States.[5] ... In 1906, the mills in Anderson had 2,575 workers who lived in the mill villages with a population in those villages totaling 6,300.

The mills in Anderson County gave housing, education, and steady employment to the unskilled rural and hill families. Fathers, mothers, and children worked in the mills. An average wage was 75 cents [per day]in 1902. ... Full time operatives worked 62 hours a week.[6]

The mill company built churches and schools in each of the villages. The mill built houses with a standard layout, identical one-story cottages for small families and two-story structures for larger ones.[7]

Each mill built commissary-type stores for their operatives, who were usually poor families that came to the mills seeking a steady source of income and needing low-cost housing and credit. The factory would assign the family a cottage and let them obtain food, clothing, and medicines on credit and subtract these expenses from the salaries of the fathers, mothers, and children at the end of each two-week payroll. The store stocked every necessity, including coffins.[8]

The Anderson Traction Company streetcar lines carried workers to and from the mills during the week.[9]

Interesting Early Visitors

In 1909, The New York Herald and Atlanta Journal's Good Roads Tour came through Anderson, its purpose being to show that one could safely drive from New York to Florida.[10]

In 1913, Teddy Roosevelt and Bill Taft came to town.[11] Amelia Earhart flew into the Anderson Airport in 1931.[12]

Chapter Two
Childhood

School

Paul's first memory is of bicycle-kicking his feet in the air while lying on his back on the bed. Why the excitement? He was finally about to start to school. Mama and big sister, Betty, were asking, "Are you ready to start to school?" Ready? He couldn't wait. He was sure he would have Miss Cochran for his teacher because Betty and older brother, Clyde, had both been in her class and had dearly loved her. School sounded like a big adventure and a lot of fun. East Whitner Street School, also called the Cleo Bailey School after the longtime principal, surely must be wonderland.

Uh oh. No Miss Cochran. Big disappointment. He consoled himself with the fact that next year he was sure to get Miss Sweetenburg, because Clyde and Betty had both been blessed with that good fortune. No such luck. When next year rolled around, the disappointment was just too much. He cried—real tears. Heartbroken, he cried and cried, but to no avail. He had Mrs. Bolt. Though he was sure the year was a total loss, Mrs. Bolt turned out to be not bad at all. In fact, she was exceptionally nice.

Riverside Baptist Church

The bus from Riverside Baptist Church came right down his street to provide a ride for anyone who would go to church. Anyone who would go? Mama would go, and she took her little flock, by now including Helen, two years younger than Paul. The bus picked them up to go the five blocks to church and delivered them back home, along with 20 or 30 other people. Church was wonderful, but the bus ride came a close second, because on the trip home, someone usually would start singing one of the hymns they had just enjoyed at church. Everyone joined in, and they sang all the way home. This was especially magical at night, to be rolling along in the dark, seeing the lights from the windows of houses, and singing the great hymns that told the Gospel story.

One especially nice thing about the church was its library. Paul, being very trustworthy for his age of seven, was allowed to take Helen with him and climb the stairs to the second floor where they would enter a room filled from top to bottom with shelves full of books.

Going to this room was just pretty much a matter of exploring to Paul, but Helen wanted books. She was not yet able to read and would need someone at home to read the books to her, and she also needed help to pick them out. He patiently fulfilled this duty. They were allowed to check them out and return them the next week. Then back down the stairs with its deep red carpet and polished mahogany rails, just in time for the service to start.

Rev. Bill Parham was a big man with a booming voice that made him a great singer as well as a preacher, and he had a big friendly smile. From his pulpit, he beamed at his parishioners while he preached, but maintained an appropriately solemn demeanor while the choir led in 15 stanzas of "Just As I Am" for the invitation to accept Jesus and be baptized. Well, it seemed like 15.

When Paul was eight, he attended a tent meeting held at Cater Lake by J. Harold Smith. Smith was a well-known and much-loved evangelist who had a radio ministry. On this particular night, he preached from 2 Kings 4:8-37 the story of Elisha and the son of the Shunammite woman. The son died, but God used Elisha to bring him back to life. As he told the story, Paul came under heavy conviction and knew he needed to accept Jesus as his Savior. He felt J. Harold Smith was speaking directly to him: not to the person in front of him or behind him, nor to the ones on either side of him. Just to him. As soon as the invitation was given, Paul hurried down the sawdust trail to the front. His pastor, Bill Parham, had been seated on the platform with some other pastors, and Parham now carefully questioned Paul to be sure he really knew what he was doing. He was satisfied with Paul's answers, so about two weeks later, he baptized this new believer in the baptismal pool at Riverside Baptist Church. Years later, Paul would preach at Riverside a few times as a lay-preacher, filling in for the pastor in his absence.

J. Harold Smith continued his ministry of evangelism, his radio ministry lasting for over 70 years.

When Paul went to school the next day, he was excited to tell his teacher what he had experienced the night before. Seeing how important it was to him, she allowed him to share the details with the class.

Now Daddy began having Paul read some verses from the Bible before going to school each morning. His love of God's written Word had begun.

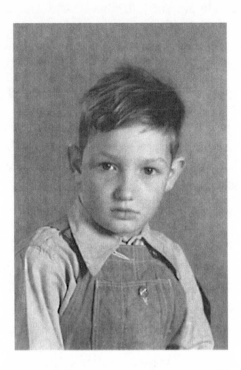

The Mill

The church was in the middle of one of the "mill villages," because the nearby mill had had the houses and the church built to accommodate the textile workers. At first the houses were only rented from the mill, but eventually the mill owners decided to allow the residents to purchase them.

Not far from the church was the Company Store. Tennessee Ernie Ford sang a song about the Company Store: "Saint Peter, don't you call me, cause I can't go. I owe my soul to the Company Store." The mill workers were allowed to charge their grocery, clothing, and medicine purchases there, because the mill that employed the people also owned the store. The charges would be subtracted from the workers' pay.

Paul's Daddy didn't work at this particular mill, and his family didn't live in the "mill village," but they benefitted from their close proximity to it. Paul and his brother and sisters made many trips to that Company Store to purchase cookies and candy, spending their nickel or dime allowance each week. In the 1940s, a nickel or dime bought a lot, especially for a little kid. There was another store Paul and his siblings passed before they got to the Company Store, this one belonging to a man known as Doc Jones. They actually spent their allowance there more than in the Company Store, but it was nice to have a choice.

The school Paul attended was provided by the mill for the many children in the "mill village." The mill also owned a large tract of wooded land, the woods through which Paul walked to school, along with a dozen or so of other children. At each end of the wooded tract was a cleared area where the mill provided a ball field. One of those ball fields was at the end of the street where Paul lived.

At one time it had sported a large section of bleachers and hosted baseball games between the mill teams, there being several mills in the town of Anderson and others in the surrounding small towns of the county. By the time Paul was nine, the bleachers had deteriorated and become unsafe, so the mill had them torn down. Still, the field was there, down a ten-foot drop, and since it was cleared, it provided a good path for part of the way to the Company Store if you chose not to go through the woods. The ball field at the other end of the wooded tract was used several years longer for ball games.

When Paul was about eleven, a teacher at the school persuaded the mill to donate one of the houses it still owned for the purpose of a neighborhood library. She was able to gather hundreds of books, and opened it to all interested persons in the surrounding area. Helen was one of those interested persons, but couldn't make that trip alone, it being several blocks away. Paul occasionally had his play interrupted to accompany her, which he did without complaint, of course. Of course.

Calvary Baptist Church

When Paul was eight, Riverside Baptist Church decided to build a mission church on a vacant lot at the other end of his block, on the corner of North and East Orr Streets. Now the bus no longer came to pick them up to go to Riverside Church. The new church, named Calvary Baptist, had a large sanctuary and many classrooms, all on one floor. It was made of concrete blocks and was situated in the center of a large sloping lot, leaving lots of room around it for parking and for playing tag or other games before and after the services. Paul and Mama became Charter Members of Calvary, and it became a very important place to Paul and the rest of his family.

Daddy had not gone with the family to Riverside church, but now took a part in the building of Calvary. His life had just undergone a drastic change. His mother, Paul's Granny Jordan, had always lived with him and had just died at the age of 80. On her deathbed, she had persuaded him to give up his occasional binge drinking and to give his life to God. Now he helped with the roofing of the new church building.

Granny Jordan

When Granny Jordan was sick near the end of her life, Paul overheard the grownups discussing what to do about her cough and congestion. A standard remedy of the time was a little bit of whiskey in lemon juice with honey. Someone suggested giving that to her. One of her daughters-in-law, Lily Mae, expressed surprise at such a suggestion. "Why, she would rather die!" That ended the consideration of this particular remedy. Granny Jordan had seen alcohol do nothing but harm, and she considered it a deadly enemy.

Granny, Ida Milford Jordan, took to her bed only two weeks before her heart failed and she died at the age of 80. Her Christian life left everyone with the confidence that she had gone to heaven. She had seen some great heartache in her 80 years. She and her twin, Emma, together with their brother, Lee, had seen their mother die when they were very young. The girls were four, and Lee was just five months.

Ida married Asa Jordan when she was 18 years old. She bore him one son, Wilton, three years later, only to see Asa die when Wilton was just one year old. She had then married her dead husband's older brother, James Berry Jordan, himself a widower with 12 children. James Berry died when Ida was 52, so she had lived as a widow for 28 years. One of her sons, Homer, had died in 1945. Now in 1948, her earthly life was over. Her casket stood in the living room of Paul's home where her children, stepchildren, grandchildren, and others gathered to mourn and comfort each other. She had been a sweet, caring grandmother to Paul and his siblings.

Bullies

When Paul was 11 and in the fifth grade at school, he began to encounter aggravation from some bullies. It was surprising that bullies would pick on him because he was always tall. Still, he was easy-going and always played fair, so perhaps they thought he wouldn't resist. Surprise! He resisted.

When W.H. wouldn't stop picking on him, Paul suggested that the two of them go into the woods by themselves and fight it out. Agreed, so off they went, though they neither one knew how to fight. W.H. swung at Paul, but missed. Next, Paul swung at him with the same result. They each tried it several more times before giving up and deciding to call it even. W.H. never bothered Paul again, maybe because he realized Paul was willing to fight back and wouldn't just let himself be run over. The two of them later became friends.

The next bully to learn a lesson from Paul was Gary. At recess one day when teams were being chosen for a baseball game, Paul had already been chosen on a team when Gary arrived. "I'm taking Paul's place on this team," he announced. "No, you are not," Paul replied. "Oh, yes I am!" he insisted. He changed his mind when he started to turn blue from the chokehold Paul placed on him. No more trouble from him, either.

One boy who went from bullying to being a great friend was Walter "Sonny" Carroll. Sonny lived at 50 North Street, while Paul lived at 83. Sonny was actually a friendly, caring person but must have been influenced for a time by his cousin who visited from Rock Hill, SC. For some reason, the cousin and Sonny chose to throw rocks at Paul and his siblings if they dared come out onto their front porch. At times they even shot at them with a BB gun. The cousin left and went home, then Sonny and Paul became great friends. The rest is history. They were friends until Sonny's death in his 50s.

Then there was Donnie, who Paul would one day have to arrest, with others to follow. Paul waited for Helen and Clyde after school to walk home (Betty was now in Junior High in a different location), but unfortunately the bullies waited in the woods for them. They told Daddy, who went to see the Principal of the school. She assured him it would be taken care of. She decided Clyde, Paul, and Helen should be let out of school at a different time from the bullies. Reasonable solution, right? Well, it could have been, but unfortunately, she let the bullies out first, so they just went to the woods to wait for their prey. If she had let Clyde, Paul, and Helen out first, they could have been long gone before the bullies ever left their seats. Now the only thing to do was avoid the shortcut through the woods and walk around the streets to get home. Through the woods was maybe a quarter of a mile, while the route around the streets was two miles. A long, tired walk at the end of a school day.

Church

Daddy now went to church with the family and was even teaching a Sunday School Class. He could be seen at home studying his Bible and making notes for what he wanted to talk about on Sunday. Unfortunately, a Church Business Meeting put an end to his attendance at this neighborhood church. Apparently the church wasn't meeting its budget requirements, so a Business Meeting was held on a Sunday night. When the pastor announced that the Deacon Board had proposed that anyone not tithing to the church be removed from the membership roll, Daddy stood up and spoke his opinion that a man had to take care of his family and might not be able to tithe. Other people then stood to voice their opinions, and the discussion became quite heated. When the pastor's wife, Betty Bowe, fainted from the stress, the discussion and the meeting ended. Many people had agreed with Daddy, but the Deacons won, and the proposal was accepted.

Daddy and the pastor, Harold Bowe, had become friends, Bowe at times coming by the house to pick Daddy up to go work on the church building. Now Daddy knew he wasn't wanted there, since he wasn't tithing. He had given some money to the church as he had felt able, and had always given Mama and the children money to put in the plate. He was hurt and felt rejected. After visiting several other churches, he now stayed home and watched preachers on TV.

When it was raining or severely cold, Daddy drove the family to church, though he no longer went himself. For many years, it was sort of a neighborhood thing for the people to walk to church together. Lula Mae lived further down the street, so she came by and walked with Mama, along with George and Marie Bratcher. Then two doors up the street, Audrey would join the group. A few more houses and Mrs. Cathay and her children joined in, then next door, Roy and Peggy Smith. Meanwhile, Paul and Clyde had several other boys in their group, and Helen and Betty had other girls. It was really a very congenial group and an enjoyable walk. When the service was over, they all walked home together, each dropping off as they arrived at their house. The exception was Paul. He usually liked to run home. Cooped up and having to be still too long? Maybe. He thought it just felt good to run, so he did. He could do it in two or three minutes.

While Paul was having trouble with bullies at school, he was having great success at church. He was deemed outstanding by his Royal Ambassador leader, Mr. Sawyer, and was presented with a special gift Bible because he had memorized many Bible verses, excelled at Sword Drills, shown a Godly character, etc.

The entire class knew about the award that was coming, and twelve-year-old Paul was sure Wade would get it. He sat and listened as Mr. Sawyer told the entire congregation how outstanding this young man he was going to recognize was and how proud he was of him. As all the exemplary characteristics were being listed, Paul was mentally agreeing: "Yep, that's Wade all right." How shocked he was when he heard Mr. Sawyer call his name and not Wade's! He was afraid to stand and take the Bible, thinking he had heard wrong.

The big contest probably came that same summer when Paul was 12—the contest the church held among the dozens of children to encourage Bible memorization. The meetings were held on Thursdays, and each week the children could recite to the teacher as many Bible verses as they had memorized that week. A grand prize would be given to the one who had memorized the most at the end of the summer. Paul was going great guns, reciting verse after verse each week. He was ahead for a long time, but Billie Jo Darby, a teenage girl, memorized the most and won the prize. Still, he had memorized and retained many verses, as he had an excellent memory that would serve him well for the rest of his life.

Simple Pleasures

Childhood for Paul in the 40s and 50s consisted of playing football and softball, hide-and-seek, cops and robbers, and marbles, damming up the nearby creek, making and flying kites, catching fireflies after dark, tying a string to a June bug's leg and letting it fly in circles, etc., all with the neighborhood kids.

Daddy said he had received wrong information about where the paved road in front of the house would be placed, so he had the house built too close to that spot, leaving a short front yard. This actually ended up being a bonus for the kids, as they had a very long backyard. In this backyard, at one point Daddy built the kids a little cart that ran on a long ramp. The cart could be pushed to the top of the four-foot-high platform, then loaded with kids, fly down across the ramp for a few feet, then back up an incline for a couple of feet and back down again to the end of the thirty-foot wooden track. A lot like a roller coaster.

Frankie Jackson, a young teenager who lived next door, helped Daddy build the cart and ramp, and Daddy, along with the rest of the family, thought a lot of him. His family moved away soon after this, and sadly he was killed in a tragic auto accident when he was just 16.

Paul's entire family grieved for him. Daddy took Paul with him to visit the family and offer condolences.

The long backyard provided ample space for ball games to be held. With Charles and Larry, Allen and Jimmy, Keith and Don, etc., there was never a shortage of players. (It seems the boys mostly came in twos.) It was a young neighborhood with most of the families having children.

They used a bat and a hard rubber ball, which would really sail when hit. Somehow the ball kept going two lots over into Mrs. Edgar's yard, and someone had to go retrieve it each time. Mrs. Edgar became annoyed with the constant running through her yard, so Paul decided on a fix for the problem. He took the family push-mower to her house and mowed her grass for her for free. He then had instant favor with her and could retrieve the ball anytime he wished. The other kids got to know her and found her to be a sweet, gentle woman who was caring for her war-damaged husband. Mr. Edgar no longer spoke, having become "shell-shocked" in the war. The Edgars were excellent, solid neighbors throughout Paul's childhood and beyond.

There was also a vacant lot across the street from Paul's house where many ball games were played. One day, Paul was the catcher but decided he didn't want to bother with wearing the catcher's mask. He soon learned what the mask was good for and what could happen if it wasn't worn. Somehow the batter happened to tip the ball backwards directly to the bridge of Paul's nose. When the bleeding stopped, the nose was a little misshapen and remained so for the rest of his life. He appreciated the mask from then on.

The family driveway, though cleared, was unpaved, so the hard dirt made a perfect surface for drawing a ring for a game of marbles. All the boys in the neighborhood (and Helen) had their collection of marbles and their special shooters. A lot of trading went on, and most of the games were not played "for keeps." That meant each player would go home with as many marbles as he had brought.

A neighbor, Mrs. Roberts, liked to go fishing but didn't like to dig up the worms for bait, so she hired Paul and Clyde to dig them for her. This brought them five cents a-piece, or if they had found a lot of worms, they might even get seven cents. Early entrepreneurial-ship.

Clyde

Paul's older brother was Clyde, born three years earlier. His was a difficult birth, and he didn't immediately breathe. This caused him to have some challenges to deal with, one being a slight mental retardation which made school difficult for him. He started school at age six, but didn't want to go, so Mama and Daddy withdrew him, planning to try again the next year. The next year when he was seven, his sister, Betty, two years younger, was sent with him to be in his class and to help him where necessary. This worked very well, as he was content now that she was there with him. He learned to read and write and was actually pretty good at math. He attended school for eight years, going through the sixth grade.

He also had a physical difficulty to deal with in the form of a leaking valve in his heart. If he ran very far, his face would take on a blue tint, and he would place his hand over his heart because of the pain there. Still, he played ball with the neighborhood kids and stuck close to Paul's side for all of the other childhood activities.

Though he was three years younger, Paul took on the role of older brother, always including Clyde and looking out for him. He waited for him after school to walk home with him. When Paul had his first car, he took Clyde with him to movies and occasionally bowling. Clyde could not have asked for a better brother.

Clyde died when he was 59. At his funeral, Paul gave a eulogy and said, "He was a little awkward, but he got the job done," whatever the job was. He was a devoted Christian, always loved his pastor, loved to watch preachers on TV, and read his Bible daily. He was good-hearted, and doing wrong or harming anyone would have been the furtherest things from his mind.

Animals

One night Daddy came home from work bringing a baby kitten. He had found it scrounging for food outside the mill, and thinking it might starve there, he decided to surprise his children with a pet. It was cute and cuddly and soon was named Bozo. This was their first pet. Daddy bought groceries from his brother Hawk's store, so he would get the ends of bologna rolls that would just be thrown away and bring them home to Bozo, who loved the meat. He spent a lot of time outdoors, being an indoor-outdoor cat. He no doubt suffered many indignities and discomforts from the handling he received from the children, they having no knowledge of the proper treatment, though they loved him dearly. Let's just say the cat ended up being bow-legged in his front two legs, and leave it at that.

A later stray cat that was adopted was called Tommy, until this cat gave birth to two kittens, it now becoming obvious to the children that this was not a Tom cat. One of the kittens had the coloring of a tiger, and was soon named Tiger Boy by Betty, who claimed him as her own.

Daddy would hold him up to the cord hanging down from the light switch and say, "Okay, Tiger Boy, turn the light on." As any cat would do when confronted with a cord, he would reach out to the cord with his paw, pull on it in an attempt to bring it to his mouth, and thereby turn the light on. "Smart cat!" Daddy would say. Tiger Boy also liked to go from one bed to the other, meowing, to wake up the family in the morning when he was ready for breakfast.

At one time Daddy fenced in the backyard and built a little barn to house three goats. The goats were interesting and fun to watch, and the goat's milk was good. Not good were the times when some neighborhood boys would open the gate, chase the goats out, then knock on the front door to inform the family, "Your goats are out!" Then the entire family would have to chase them down, sometimes for blocks. The goats were Olympic-speed runners. The culprits who had opened the gate and chased the goats out were probably having great fun watching the family run after them. Eventually the goats were sold and pigs took their place.

After the pigs had become sausage, Daddy bought a cow, Bessie. Bessie had to be led to the woods each morning, where she would spend the day grazing with other cows that belonged to neighbors. Daddy worked the second shift at the mill, from three to eleven, so at the end of the day, just before dark, Mama would go get Bessie and lead her home, back to her little barn. There she gave milk for the family. Some of the milk was churned, making delicious butter. A short rope around Bessie's neck was all Mama needed with which to guide her home, but when Paul would insist on leading her, she resisted and would try to bite him. She had her favorites, and he wasn't one of them.

After Bessie came Nicey, who led the same life. Then came the era of chickens. Lots of chickens. Paul had a pet rooster who would follow him around and craved his attention. Paul would hold him, stroking his feathers, and talk to him. In the late afternoon, the rooster would find Paul, knowing he would place him on a limb of a tree for roosting through the night. When it was the rooster's time to become Sunday dinner, the family just couldn't eat him, so he was given to some neighbors. All of the chickens were eventually killed, plucked, and taken to the city's food freezer, where they were brought out one by one for delicious fried chicken each Sunday.

On a number of occasions the backyard boasted a garden. In reality, the family had all of the elements of a farm, except the elements came one at the time.

Conscience

Paul had a well-developed conscience while growing up. One day he, Charles, and Larry had an argument with Jimmy, who lived in a house behind Paul's. The argument intensified to the point that rocks were being thrown from one side of the fence to the other. Charles was especially adept at sailing a flat rock and hitting his target. This time his target was Jimmy, the rock striking him near the temple and causing a lot of bleeding. Instantly, Paul felt sorry for him and felt horrible about what he had been doing. He ran to the house and told Mama, "I need a 'whuppin.'" "For what?" she asked. Paul told her what they had been doing and about Jimmy being injured, so Mama broke a switch from a tree and gave him a few licks. "That's not enough," he cried, "do more." So she did until he was satisfied that the punishment had fit the crime.

Grandparents' House

When Paul was in the sixth grade, Mama also went to work on the second shift at the mill. She had worked for several years in the mill before, so this time she was training new employees. She and Daddy had to be at work by 3 PM, so the children had to get out of school a little early to be picked up and carried to Grandmother's house across town. Mama would have a snack for them in the car. They would play outside until dark, eat supper, then a little later be put to bed to sleep until they were awakened after 11 PM to be carried home. They usually would go back to sleep in the car and have to be awakened again when they got home.

Playing outside, they met new friends in Grandmother's neighborhood. The next-door neighbor had a prolific apple tree and told the kids they could have all the apples that fell on the ground. They took her up on her offer. Many apples fell, and they were delicious.

Paul and Clyde played with Gene and Charles in the big field behind Grandmother's house and would often walk the four blocks to Uncle Roy's and get him to go with them one block back to the ballpark the Appleton Mill provided. There they played ball with Uncle Roy and the other boys who had gathered there.

Mama only worked a few months, but Daddy saved the money she made and built a neighborhood grocery store in the big backyard. A street with seven houses on it ran by the side of the house and down to a dead end at the creek, and the store faced that street.

The store had a gas pump as well as a kerosene pump, many people using kerosene to start fires in addition to using it in lamps. The store became employment for Clyde, but each of the family members worked in it at some time. No more ballgames in the backyard, no more animals, no more garden. No more afternoon trips to Grandmother's after school, because Mama was no longer working.

Daddy also opened a grocery store on S. McDuffie Street and hired a young man to run it for him. This didn't last too long, and he closed it, but the store in the backyard lasted for many years.

Paul would take the family push-mower and the sling blade and cut the lawns of several neighbors to earn money. He had to cut the grass in his own yard, too, of course, but he always looked for other yards to cut, for which he would be paid. Always a hard worker, no one ever found fault with his work.

Chapter Three
Teen Years

The Bible in School!

Paul's ability to memorize Bible passages continued to be exemplary, and he later memorized most of the book of James as well as other long passages. He was also excellent at Sword Drills, the contest to see who could find a passage first when the teacher called out the location in the Bible. Paul loved this activity and told his seventh-grade teacher about how much fun it was. She then allowed her class to conduct these Bible Drills in her classroom during the homeroom period, using the time period she had previously been spending having a Daily Devotional. At first Paul was the one to call out the location of the verse to be found, but soon others wanted to do the calling, so Paul got to compete. It wasn't long before almost all of the students would bring their Bibles to class and participate, giving Paul some stiff competition to be first. This surely must have had a very positive impact on the rest of their lives.

This teacher even gave her students a spelling test on the books of the Bible. Her star Bible student, Paul, was embarrassed that he only made 92 on the test. Pretty good, really, as spelling never was his strong suit.

The teacher grew to respect Paul's knowledge of the Bible and probably believed he would one day become a great preacher. When some members of the class were killed in a car wreck, some of the girls became very emotional and needed counseling and comfort. The teacher asked Paul to talk with them, thinking that he would be able to offer great comfort because of his knowledge of the Bible. Unfortunately, his words were sorely lacking in comfort: "We all have to die sometime," he told them. Louder crying, more tears. His counseling skills needed work.

First Love

When he was in the eighth grade, he spotted what he thought must be the prettiest girl in the whole world, Leora Payne. Though she was older, in the ninth grade, he would not be deterred. He was so smitten he thought his heart would burst. After seeing her in the halls a number of times, he decided to write her a note. He was so shy he couldn't possibly face her and deliver the note himself, so he got his friend, Wendell Strickland, to deliver it for him. It worked! She wrote him back! Notes began flying back and forth. He was thrilled. She didn't seem to notice when the flavor of the notes changed, that happening because Paul now had Mal Cromer writing them for him. Wendell still was the delivery boy, of course.

Paul would call her on the phone and talk to her but was still too shy to speak to her face to face. Sixty years later, he still remembers her phone number: 225-8392.

One day, the most unbelievable thing happened. As he was walking down the hall, he noticed Leora and several other people standing side by side across the hallway, leaving a small space where one could squeeze by. As he squeezed into the open space, she suddenly fell into his arms. He thought he had died and gone to heaven. He quickly stood her up on her feet and hurried away, never saying a word. He couldn't speak, so he just walked on down the hall. She must have thought she could force some conversation out of him with this stunt, but no such luck. The notes continued as usual, though. She gave him a 5 x 7 framed picture of herself, and Paul, thinking he might damage it, asked Sonny to carry it for him. Bad move, as Sonny sat on it and broke the glass into a thousand pieces.

For several years afterwards, she sent him birthday cards, and they sent each other Christmas cards. About 20 years later, he was a Deacon at Fellowship Baptist Church where her brother was the Song Leader. One night, there she was. Paul shook hands with her, the only time he ever dared touch her except the time she had fallen into his arms. She had married Aubrey Pearson, a boy Paul had known well in his teens.

Aubrey Pearson

Aubrey had a Snowball route and pushed his cart through Paul's neighborhood. When Paul was 13 or 14, he somehow got on Aubrey's bike and rode it up toward the church at the end of the block. Coming back, the Cathays' dog chased him down the hill near the creek and caused him to fall, damaging the bike. When Aubrey saw the damage, he became furious and grabbed Paul in a wrestling hold. They fell to the ground in the street, Paul on top. The next thing he knew, Mama had run out of the house with a switch and let him feel a few blows. She broke up the fight.

Years later Aubrey, who now had a well-drilling company, came to drill a well at Paul's daughter's house. When he asked who her father was and she told him Paul Jordan, he said, "Oh, yeah. I know him. We once got into a fight growing up." He drilled a good well for Paula, anyway.

Get a Job

When he was 16, Paul decided he either wanted to be a preacher or a policeman. He went downtown to the Police Department and asked the Chief for guidance to prepare for a career in Law Enforcement. Were there any courses he could take in school that would help prepare him for this job? No. All he had to do was be 21 and apply.

Daddy thought he should get a job in the mill where he worked, so he took him in for an interview. His answers to some questions put an end to a job possibility there. Did he have a back problem? Did his back hurt? He remembered that during horseplay, Don Sawyer had pushed him off the Sawyers' high porch a short while earlier, and yes, his back still hurt some from this. He also was dizzy at times, he said. He was turned down for the job. Daddy was incredulous when he asked Paul about what had transpired and Paul innocently told him what he had told the interviewer. "You shouldn't have told him that!" Well, Paul didn't want to work in the mill, anyway.

Daddy did take him to a Chiropractor after this to have his back checked out. The Chiropractor found it very misaligned, and explained that he certainly had cause for pain in his back. Then he did treatments to try and correct the problem.

Henry J

Paul's friend, Sonny, had a Henry J. that was in pretty pitiful shape but could be persuaded to run with a little effort. Sonny would tie a rope to the gearshift and hang the rope out the window. He and Paul would push the car while in neutral, then when it reached a certain speed, Sonny would pull the rope to change gears, then quickly jump inside to keep it going. It had its faults, but it was a car. They just about wore it the rest of the way out running it up and down their street.

Western Union

Paul's friend, Dalton, had a job delivering telegrams for Western Union, and as he was ready to quit that job, he told Paul that would be a good job for him. Paul had a bike, so he applied and got the job delivering telegrams after school and on the weekends.

He reported to work at 5 PM and delivered telegrams all over town. There were usually less than 10 to be delivered during his shift, which ended at 10 PM. He had no break for dinner, so he could eat before 5 and after he returned home after 10. He was given street directions before he left the Western Union office, but finding the right house was sometimes difficult after dark. One night, after dark, he was in the black section of town, a place that was unfamiliar and a little uncomfortable, and was trying to locate the correct house. He asked a woman who was walking down the street where the Lees lived. "It's right down the street here," she said, as she threw her arm around his neck, walking along by his bike in the pitch-black dark. "Come on, you can go with me down there," she continued. After a few steps, she turned to him and asked, "Are you black or white?" Paul said that if he had told the truth he would have said, "I'm yellow," but he managed to avoid giving a direct answer. They reached the house, he thanked her, delivered the telegram, jumped back on his bike, and gratefully left the area. A couple of blocks away, he made a wrong turn but soon realized it and doubled back, heading back to the office.

After he graduated from Boys High School, he was promoted to the Western Union office in Aiken, SC as an operator. The position required the worker to be able to type 40 words a minute, which Paul could not do. Unfortunately but fortunately, Paul had been stung by a bee right between the eyes just days before he needed to take the typing test. His face was so swollen that his eyes were almost shut. He said he made 40 mistakes in 38 words, but it didn't matter. The person administering the test assumed he couldn't possibly see with his eyes so swollen, so he reported that Paul had done okay. He was given the job.

The Manager in Aiken, a middle-aged woman, worked the morning shift, and Paul worked the afternoon, their work overlapping by just one hour. He was grateful it was only an hour each day, as she was very difficult to work with. His only title was Operator, but since there were only two employees and he knew he wasn't the Manager, he told the girls he met at church that he was the Assistant Manager. Sounded nice. They were impressed.

Most of the messages could be delivered by phone, then the paper copy could just be mailed to the recipients. Senator Strom Thurmond had an office in the courthouse, so a number of times Paul had messages to deliver to him. He occasionally had to deliver bad news about a death and hear the painful, shocked cries on the other end of the line. After he had delivered the bad news via phone to one woman, he couldn't stop thinking that there must be a better way than just bluntly reading what the message said. This particular woman was expecting a sick brother to die, but the news was that her other brother had died. She was stunned when he read her the message, but he had no choice. He wondered how he would have felt receiving such unexpected news. Sometimes the job was very unpleasant.

He lived in a boarding house where $20 a week bought him three meals a day, except only two on Sunday. After nine months, he was home in Anderson for a visit when he decided he wouldn't go back. Sonny was with him as he prepared to call the Manager to inform her he wasn't coming back. He kept telling Sonny, "Don't you let me agree to go back. You make me stick to my guns, no matter what she says." She was most unhappy, to say the least, and though she couldn't find fault with his work, on his reference she stated: "Left his job while he was still needed."

He had travelled to Aiken by bus, as he didn't have a car. He sent money home to Mama and Daddy, just to be helpful to them. He didn't realize until he came home that they had saved the money and bought him a car.

Chapter Four
Adulthood

Marines

Dalton had just been killed in a car wreck, and his brother, Bobby, needed his mind occupied with something else and a change of scenery. He had been thinking a lot about the Marines, so now seemed the right time to join. He travelled to Greenville, SC, there being no Recruitment Center in Anderson, and signed up for the Marine Reserves. This would entail six months of training, then one weekend a month plus two weeks in the summer.

He told Paul what he had done and tried to persuade him to join, as well. Paul said he'd have to think about it. When Bobby started to persuade, he never let up. Pretty soon he had Paul convinced, so he travelled to Greenville, too. Soon they were headed for Parris Island, SC for the training.

Paul's injury occurred not far into the training. He felt the pain in his ankle and tried to ignore it, but soon the foot was so swollen he couldn't get his boot on. He reported to Sick Bay. Off to Beaufort to the hospital, where they x-rayed and found not just a break, but a bad one. Here his foot and leg were put in a cast, and he was placed on bed rest. He remained there for six weeks, then was released to return to training. After nine days, the ankle broke again. Back to the hospital, back in a cast, for five weeks this time. After the doctors gave their opinions to the officers in charge, an officer visited Paul with an offer. The doctors felt it would take a long time for the ankle to heal properly, so the Marines presented three choices: wait six months and then try the Army, their training not deemed to be as stringent, wait two years and then try the Marines again, or just leave with an Honorable Discharge. Paul felt he needed to get on with life and not be simply waiting, so he chose the Honorable Discharge. At age 75,

Paul still has to wear special shoes and has a boney projection where the break occurred.

Hotel

Back in Anderson, he became the Night Auditor at the Calhoun Hotel. The year was 1959, and he was 19. He handled the Posting Machine, totaled the receipts from the restaurant and the hotel itself, and made up the day's deposit. The money had to match the receipts to the penny. One night, someone managed to steal some money from the cash drawer while he was on duty. He was puzzled as to who would have done such a thing. Still, he was responsible for the money on his watch, so without saying anything to anyone, he made up for the loss of $40, which was a large part of his meager pay.

Later some money was missing from a charitable fund. Paul and the hotel manager were the two who handled the money.

His boss asked him what seemed to be a rhetorical question: "Paul, what would you do if you had something to do that you really didn't want to do?" Paul's answer: "I would just do it." "Right," the man said, "well, I have to fire you because of the missing money. I don't think you took it, but I have no choice."

Paul had been out of work, drawing unemployment, for three or four weeks when the boss called and asked him to come back. The manager of the hotel had been caught stealing other money, so it was realized that he, not Paul, had taken the money from the fund.

Paul worked this job at night and began working for the American Home Insurance Company during the day. To say he was always sleepy would be an understatement. When he asked his boss at the hotel for a raise and the boss said he couldn't afford it, Paul gave his notice and quit. He had counted the money each night and had seen that a raise was certainly feasible and was very disappointed that his boss had given that excuse.

He continued with the insurance company, but soon also got a job as Desk Clerk at the Holiday Inn.

Dates

Bobby was dating a girl named Lucy. Bobby was cocky about how devoted to him Lucy was and bragged about it. He was sure nobody could entice her away from him, but he wanted to prove it to Paul. He told Paul to call and ask her for a date. "No way. I don't want to date her," Paul answered. When Bobby kept insisting and insisting, Paul asked, "What if she says 'yes'?" "She won't. That's what I'm trying to tell you. She's so crazy about me, she wouldn't date anybody else. Now go call her." Paul finally gave in and called her. When he asked for a date, she said, "Sure!" Bobby was stunned. Paul was stuck. He couldn't stand her up, but he didn't want to go.

With a heavy heart he picked her up for the date. Not wanting to hurt her feelings, he asked her for another date. Then another. In the meantime, Bobby was mad at him. Paul had stolen his girl. How could a good friend do such a thing?

Love of His Life

While Paul was dating her one night, Bobby met a girl he was very attracted to named Paulette. He immediately asked her for a date. She was with her friend, Frances, and Paulette wanted him to get her a date, too. No need to stay mad at Paul, now that he needed him, he thought. Paul agreed to date this Frances, and the rest is history. Frances Elizabeth Ellison was now the prettiest girl he had ever seen. At this writing, he and Frances, the love of his life, have been married 52 years. Bobby and Paulette also married and have been together for the same amount of time.

Chapter Five
Policeman

On April 4, 1963, at age 23, Paul married Frances, who was just 19. Now he applied at the Police Department and waited to see if he would be hired, meanwhile still working at the Holiday Inn. A year later, his sister-in-law saw his name in the paper stating that the City Council had hired him for the Police Department. It was news to him, good news. He finally would get to do what he had wanted to do for years. As soon as he could that afternoon, he went to the Police Department, was sent to a tailor shop to have a uniform fitted, was issued a badge and a gun, and told to report to work the next afternoon.

Daily Mail   Anderson, S. C., Tues., July 14, 1964   7

PAUL T. JORDAN   W. LARRY LARK   J. M. (BUCK) HOOPER

NEW POLICEMEN ON FORCE HERE

Three new members of the Anderson Police Department who are serving three-month probation terms are pictured above. They were elected to fill vacancies on the department. All three are graduates of Boys High. Ptl. Paul T. Jordan, 24, of 605 Lee St., was a clerk at the Holiday Inn. He served in the Marines. Ptl. W. Larry Lark, 34, of 302 Mayfield Dr., was an MP in the Army and formerly was employed in Belton with a finance company. Ptl. J. M. Hooper, 24, of 193 Sumter St., was affiliated with his father in the TV repair business. He attended the Atlanta School of Electronics. Ptl. Hooper was born in Banks County, Ga. The others are natives of Anderson. (Daily Mail photos by Kayle Turner).

Back then, there was no Academy in Columbia for training. The Chief just put all new hires on Church Street. Church Street would sift them out. Those who couldn't take it, quit. Those who stuck it out, well, they stayed around for more.

The Chief told him he would be trained while on duty, a real "hands on" kind of training. He would shortly get a really good glimpse of what that training would be like.

There were four beats: South, Hotel, Tolly, and Depot. He was assigned to the South Beat, which included Church Street, a street with 11 beer joints in one block. He soon thought he was on the set of a Western movie. For his first week, he was assigned with a veteran officer, Horace Marrett. On Paul's first day, they arrested seven who were drunk and disorderly, one who was threatening people with a knife, and one for a shooting.

On weekend evenings, Church Street got what was called the "Rat Patrol." This was made up of six policemen instead of the usual one, and they all got extra pay for this special duty. Let's just say weekend evenings on Church Street were active for police work.

Sometime later Paul was working Church Street alone. He had walked the beat and was on the corner when he heard a shot. As he turned toward the sound, someone ran toward him shouting, "A man's been shot!" As he hurried after the one who had come to get him, he spotted a man lying in the street, shot in the abdomen. The man who had run to get him continued, "He's in there! The one who did it is in there!" He was pointing toward a beer joint.

He stayed at Paul's side as they entered the building. There was a crowd inside the dimly-lit building, and Paul asked him, "Which one?" "The one coming toward you!" Paul looked, and it seemed they ALL were coming toward him. "Which one?" he asked again. The man jumped in front of him and pointed at the face of a big man in the front of the crowd. "That's him! He did it! He did it!" Paul stepped forward, saying, "You're under arrest" and reached to apprehend the man, who, fortunately, did not resist.

Now this you won't believe. The Police Department didn't use handcuffs, so Paul had nothing with which to restrain the prisoner.

He put his hand inside the man's belt in the middle of his back and steered him out the door, around the corner, through an alley, onto the parking lot of the Police Station, and finally through the door where the Chief of Police was inside. As Paul began explaining to the Chief what had happened, the Chief began to frisk the prisoner. It only took him a moment to pull the pistol from the man's pocket, wave it in Paul's face, and admonish him to be more careful in the future.

If Paul had had time to think, he would have realized the man probably had a gun on his person somewhere because he had just shot someone. With just the two of them going through the alley, the man could have jumped Paul at any time, shot him, and escaped.

In the meantime, Billy Newton had taken the wounded man in a patrol car to the Emergency Room at the hospital, where he was treated for his wound and lived to fight another day.

Not long after this, Paul went to the Army-Navy store and purchased for himself a pair of handcuffs for eight dollars. Other policemen would then call Paul when they had apprehended a prisoner and say, "Come and bring your handcuffs." Soon two or three other policemen bought their own, and before long the department began issuing them to all the men.

This was 1964, not the Dark Ages. There was no training for the new recruits, and they were sent out to the worst beat to patrol, with no handcuffs. Hard to believe. A wonder any rookie cop survived. After the first week, Horace Marrett patrolled with Paul on the weekends, being joined in the evenings by others in the "Rat Patrol," but during the week, he was alone.

After several men jumped Horace when he was alone, beat him, and took his badge and gun, the Chief decided that two men should always be together.

Well, now Paul understood what the Chief meant by being trained on duty.

The New Cop

Why did the man not resist arrest but go peacefully with Paul to the Police Station? Obviously, God protected Paul, but in addition, Paul's reputation had already been established.

In his first week at work, he had come upon a crowd that had gathered around a cat in the street that had been hit by a car. The crowd had watched to see what he would do. When he saw the cat couldn't possibly survive, he chose to put it out of its misery. A quick death would be the most merciful thing, so he pulled out his Black Jack, the Billy Club, and with one swift blow ended the cat's pain. Murmurs from the crowd as they backed away from him. So that's how this new cop would handle things—a swift use of force. Better not buck him.

That same day his reputation was enhanced. As he patrolled, he was told about a man who had passed out in one of the beer joints. The owner wanted the man out of there. The crowd outside saw Paul go in, but they couldn't see what was going on inside. When Paul came dragging the intoxicated man out of the joint, they surmised that he had clubbed him, too. More backing away, more determination not to buck this new guy. Paul never had any trouble out of the crowd that loitered on the sidewalks of Church Street. Ironically, when Paul ended his police career eight and a half years later, he had never used his club on any person. He had found that if he treated the people the way he would want to be treated, they didn't resist arrest.

Murder

Paul had started his Police career on June 6th of 1964, and on July 5th, almost a month later, he was riding in a Patrol Car with veteran officer, Harold Huff. Just musing, Paul asked Harold how long he thought it would be before he would see someone who had been killed. Harold said confidently, "You'll see one before the month is out." "Before the month is out? This is the last day," Paul thought. Turned out, Harold knew what he was talking about.

That night before their shift was over, Paul and Harold got a call to go to the Anderson Hospital parking lot to see what was going on, as an incident had been reported. The Radio Operator, Jim Burris, later to become Chief of Police, gave the call to Paul and Harold, but two officers riding in another car also heard the call. Those two, Captain Billy Newton and Buck Hooper, an old friend of Paul's, apparently were bored and wanted to take the call instead. They contacted Paul and asked, "What's your 1020?" "We're on Market Street," Paul replied. "We're closer to the hospital. We'll take the call," Buck said.

Harold and Paul didn't have anything going on, and besides, Jim had given them the call, so they decided to go, too. The first thing Paul saw was a woman, covered in blood, standing beside a station wagon. He thought, "Oh, man, she's really been hurt!" Turned out, she wasn't hurt at all, but the man she was with had been knifed 26 times by her jealous husband. She was now covered in that man's blood.

Her husband had been placed in the back seat of the other patrol car, and Captain Billy Newton told Paul to get in with him and keep an eye on him. As he got in, the man began spilling his story, admitting to the knifing.

Paul and Harold carried him to jail, while the wounded man was being carried into the hospital. Leaving the jail, Paul and Harold decided to go back to the hospital and see what more was happening. When they arrived, they found the wounded man had been pronounced dead. Harold had been right: Paul would see someone killed before his first month at work was over. It was four hours till the end of his shift when the month would be up. As Paul looked at the dead man's face, he regretted even asking about seeing someone killed. Death seemed a terrible enemy. He thought of what the Bible said about life and death, that life is but a vapor, appearing for a short time and then vanishing away.

The police learned that the man who had been killed had some pretty rough sons, and it was feared they would storm the jail to seek revenge on the man who had killed their father. Paul and Harold had to transfer the prisoner to the county jail at 7 AM because that jail had better security. Finally, at 8 AM, his shift was over and he could go home to try and sleep. Sleep was elusive, though. It had been a jarring experience.

Foster Parents

One day at work, Paul was told to go to a beer joint across the street from the Police Department to answer a complaint from the owner. The owner had called to say that a very drunk woman was in his establishment, and he wanted her removed. When Paul arrived, he found the woman's 13-year-old son was with her. The son's name was Jack [not his real name]. He told Paul, "If you lock her up, she has to be out by 3 or 4 to cook for my younger brother and sister." Paul had no choice but to lock her up until she was sober. Jack went home to take care of his younger siblings.

In the meantime, Paul and Frances were being approved by the Department of Social Services to be foster parents.

Their first foster child was Randy [not his real name], an eleven-year-old diabetic. His mother loved him but would give him anything he wanted to eat, and as a result, his diabetes was out of control. The courts placed him in foster care, but because of his medical condition, no family had accepted him. When Paul and Frances learned of his situation, they decided to take him. They knew it would not be easy, as he needed a special diet and extra care. Frances carefully cooked his meals according to his diabetic guidelines, and Paul encouraged him to exercise by doing the exercises with him. He had him doing the exercises he had learned during his brief stint in the Marines: pushups, situps, side straddle hops, etc. Randy was with them for two years, then went to live with his sister for a while. After this, he was in two other foster homes, neither of which worked well for him. Finally, he came back to Paul and Frances.

Next came Jack, the thirteen-year-old who had been with his mother when Paul locked her up until she could become sober. Along with him was his sister, Sarah, and his brother, Buddy [not their real names]. Paul feared Jack would be resentful because of his arresting his mother and would not want to live with them, but Jack assured him that he understood Paul had only done what was necessary. Paul's standard was to always treat everyone the way he would want to be treated, so Jack had seen him treat his mother kindly, even in her drunken state.

Next came another group of siblings: Jay, Chuck, and Carly [not their real names]. Now they had seven foster children, which they kept for five years. Later they took care of others, for a total of 13, two of which were babies less than a month old.

They took them to church and gave them Godly role models. Before bedtime each night, they had Family Devotions, reading from the Bible, sharing, and praying. They helped with homework and went to the school for teacher conferences when needed. The nine of them, Paul, Frances, and the seven children, made a good baseball team. They would go to the park and challenge the group of boys playing ball there to a real game. Jay was an outstanding player, and the others did well, so the foster children with Paul and Frances usually won! Being part of a team, especially a winning team, was a great morale booster for the children, helping to repair their self-esteem. When Jack was 14 and Jay 15, they cut the grass in 30 or 40 yards to earn money, all of which they were allowed to keep. How fortunate these kids were to have been placed with Paul and Frances.

Years later Paul would write in a newspaper article, "I can close my eyes and see the old ball field we used to play on during the summer, my wife, myself, and the seven foster children. It's hard looking back, knowing things will never be the same again. Time moves on, and we must move with it."

Night Shift

When Paul worked the night shift, his hours were from 12 Midnight until 8 AM. From 12 to 1, he would have to "shake the doors" on the stores on his beat, then ride in the Patrol Car from 1 to 5, returning to shake the doors again from 5 to 8, making sure no unauthorized persons had entered. He was surprised at how many merchants would end their workday and forget to lock the door to their store.

When Paul worked the night shift, he had difficulty sleeping in the daytime with children in the house. By now, he and Frances had two daughters: Kimberly Ann, born Dec. 28, 1968 and Paula Denise, born Sept. 19, 1971. It was impossible and would have been unfair to keep the girls completely quiet while he tried to sleep. When Paul mentioned to Daddy that he didn't know what to do in order to get some sleep, Daddy took it upon himself to convert Paul's garage to an extra bedroom, and there he slept very well. Daddy also came to the rescue when Paul's flat-roofed house leaked. Paul had employed a roofer to repair it, but it still leaked. Daddy decided the roof had to be elevated to permanently fix the problem, so he purchased the materials, did the work, and leaking was a thing of the past.

One night Paul was patrolling downtown on foot about 11 PM, when a cow that had gotten loose came running through town with a young man on a motor scooter chasing it. Paul called the station to report this and was told to round it up if he could. He didn't have a patrol car, so he ran over to the Yellow Cab stand and asked if they had seen which way the cow had gone. One driver had and told Paul to hop in.

Off they went in hot pursuit. Turning off Whitner Street onto Tower, they soon found the cow lying in the road and the car that had hit it—Daddy's car. He had just gotten off from work and was driving home when the cow ran right in front of him, giving him no time to even brake. Daddy's chest was bruised from striking the steering wheel, but the cow was ready for the butcher. Daddy called a lawyer, who told him to take possession of the cow to compensate for the damage to his car, in case they couldn't find the owner.

Daddy called a butcher, who came and butchered the cow on the concrete of the service station lot next to the site of the accident. The cab took Paul back to the Police Station where he got his personal car and returned to stay with Daddy until everything was finished. They finally got to go home about 3 AM. The meat was packaged and frozen, and Daddy was able to sell enough to pay for his car repairs.

The young man on the motor scooter had no connection to the cow. He had just spotted it and decided to have fun chasing it.

The cow's owner was never found.

Daddy and Kim

Daddy had been out of church for many years. One day he took Paul's little three-year-old daughter, Kim, with him to the cemetery, where he faithfully took care of his mother's grave. His mother was the one who, on her deathbed, had convinced him to give up his occasional binge drinking and accept Jesus as Savior.

Now at her grave, Kim pointed to a nearby statue and told him, "Look, there's Jesus!" The excitement and reverence in her voice caught his attention, as he turned to look where she was pointing. What he saw seemed more than a statue, as Jesus became very real to him. His heart was touched, changed. Repentant, he returned to God with his whole heart.

With tears flowing, he told Paul what had happened, trying to explain the supernatural encounter he had experienced. Jesus was very close to him for the rest of his life—which was only one year.

The Scripture in Isa. 11:6 was real: a little child had led him, and led him just in time.

Sir Galahad

One day Paul was walking a beat downtown when Frances came to see him. It had been raining, and there was a puddle Frances would have to cross to get to him. He later thought that he could have just picked her up and lifted her over the puddle, but that didn't occur to him at the time. Instead, he stood in the puddle and told her to step on his shoe, which she did.

Someone was watching and walked over to tell him, "That wasn't exactly how Sir Galahad would have done it, but it sure was okay!"

Shooting

One day a call came in to the station that two men had stolen a car in Augusta, GA and were seen heading toward Anderson. Someone spotted the car parked behind the Recreation Center, but the men were nowhere in sight. Captain Billy Newton posted Paul and Bob Edson, along with two other policemen, in stake-out positions around the car. About two hours later, the two men came back for the car. Paul and Bob both yelled, "Police! Stop!" One man ran, but the other one pulled a gun from his belt, raised and cocked it. Before he could shoot, both Paul and Bob shot at him, wounding him in the arm. They then took him into custody. Neither Paul nor Bob could tell which one of them had hit the man, they were just glad they could capture him. The Chief told them, "One of you is a very good shot. The other needs to go to the range and practice."

Twenty-five years later, Paul was selling insurance and knocked on a door in Greenville. When a man came to the door, Paul said, "Independent Life Insurance." The man carefully studied his face, then said, "Anderson Police Department." Paul said, "No, Independent Life Insurance." The man then insisted, "No, Anderson Police Department. You shot me in the arm." Paul had not recognized him, but he had never forgotten Paul's face.

Overkill

One day Paul was told to come pick up a man a Highway Patrolman had stopped, and take him to the jail, as he was very drunk. When Paul arrived, he found it hard to breathe, the smell of Mace was so strong. He thought the Patrolman must have saturated the man with the stuff. It was bad enough when the man was out in the open air, but closed up in Paul's patrol car, the effects were unbearable. Paul's eyes burned terribly, making it difficult to see. He managed to drive back to the Station by keeping his head out the window the entire way.

Creative Tactic

When someone who was out of control was brought into the station or into the Emergency Room at the Hospital, Paul was sent to talk to them and calm them down. One night he was at the desk in the

Station when the phone rang. When he answered it, a man's voice said, "I'm about to kill myself." Instead of trying to talk him out of it, which might or might not have worked, Paul used a different tactic. "Okay," he said, "just let me get the facts for my report." "Report?" the man said, "What report?" "Oh, we have to keep records. We have to have all the details for the report. Now, who are you and where are you?" Paul continued, signaling for another policeman to get the information as he wrote it down. The other policeman radioed a patrol car in the area and told the policemen what was happening. "How do you plan to do this?" Paul asked next. "Do you have a gun, or do you plan to overdose on pills?" "This is crazy," the man said. "Why are you asking me these questions? I'm serious. I'm going to do it." "Okay," Paul said. "Just let me get the details for my report first." The man kept talking and answering questions as long as Paul kept asking. Now the Police arrived at his house, a nearby preacher who had been notified arrived, and the man was peacefully taken into custody. There would be no suicide that night.

Line of Duty

One night Paul arrested a man who was coming from Starr, driving erratically. Paul followed him for a short time, then pulled him over and charged him with DUI. When the man's court date came up, Paul was called in to testify. The man had hired a lawyer who was determined to get his client off. The lawyer would ask Paul a question about the arrest, but never allow him to complete his answer. The man got off as not guilty. Seeing this happen again and again, Paul then simply drove some drunks home rather than arrest them and have them go to court. Still, most of the arrests he performed during his eight and a half years as a Policeman were for the charges of being Drunk in Public or Drunk and Disorderly.

Any time someone Paul had arrested appeared in court for trial, Paul had to be present to testify. This would happen two or three times a week. This wasn't a great inconvenience if he was working the morning shift, because he could go to court while on duty. If he had worked the afternoon shift, from 4 to 12, or the night shift, from 12 to 8, it took a chunk out of his off-duty time to have to come in to testify. This testifying was done without pay for the time consumed, of course.

Sometimes Paul rode in the patrol car with a Lt. who was somewhat of a slow driver. At the end of four hours of driving, he would have travelled only 14 miles. Other policemen continually teased him that he was helping anyone thinking of breaking into a store. The potential thief could see him drive by, knowing he wouldn't be back for hours, and have plenty of time to do a thorough job of a robbery. Captain Billy Newton, however, was known to drive by one block, then quickly double back, occasionally catching a thief who had thought he had lots of unobserved time to do his dirty deed.

Many people think policemen only like to eat donuts and drink coffee, those items being free to them from the donut establishments. The Anderson police had a better deal—fried chicken. The workers at KFC would call the station and say, "Come see the Colonel," so someone would go pick up the chicken. Finger-lickin' good.

Anderson's Otis

Mayberry had its Otis, and Anderson had its Hiram [not his real name]. Hiram officially lived with his sister, but he spent most of his nights in the jail sleeping off his alcohol consumption. On the first of the month when he received his VA benefits check, he could pay his bail and get out. Otherwise, he stayed. One day he paid his bail and got out, only to be locked up a few hours later for public drunkenness, paid his way out again, then was locked up a third time in the same day for the same offense. When he went before the Judge, the Judge decided he should have only been charged bail once, as he should have been kept all day to sober up.

He had a friend named Peters [not his real name] who drank with him and enjoyed the same kind of accommodations at the jail. Neither one of them got into fights or destroyed property when they were drunk, but they couldn't be allowed to loiter about on the streets in that condition, not to mention how unsafe it was for them to stagger about in traffic. Locking them up was the most humane thing to do, and they never seemed to mind.

One day Paul and the Chief had been having coffee at a café near the Police Station. When they walked out onto the sidewalk, Hiram came up to Paul and started talking. Paul turned to the Chief and said, "I can't tell when he's drunk and when he's not," to which the Chief replied, "Well, he's at least half drunk. Take him to jail and charge him half a fine." (Joking, of course.)

The Green House

On the square there was a small 5ft. by 5ft. building, called the "Green House." This was a glass house, framed with wood painted green, placed there to let a policeman get in out of a terrible downpour or severely cold weather. All sides were glass, allowing him to see in all directions. Inside was a small heater that would help him thaw out on cold winter days, when he stepped inside for a few minutes. He couldn't stay long, as he had to cover his beat, but at times it was a lifesaver.

On a pole in front of the "Green House" was a phone with a direct line to the Police Station. This was an extension of the Station's phone, so it couldn't be used to call anywhere else. Anyone trying to use it for a personal call would be surprised to hear the police dispatcher asking what he wanted. It could be used to notify the Station of the need for backup when something occurred that one policeman alone couldn't handle. It gave a measure of security to the policeman on the beat, knowing contact could be made so quickly. By 1968 or '69, the Department issued "walkie-talkies" to the men, and communication became easier.

Gun Shots

One night around 11 PM, Paul and his partner were told to go to Fulmer Street where a man was shooting a gun into the air. They wanted to approach without being spotted by the crowd in the street, so they pulled behind a house to park and observe. They wanted to try and spot the shooter and catch him red-handed. When headlights flashed on their patrol car and immediately a station wagon sped away, they realized this was the man who had been shooting and that he had spotted them. They gave chase. Going at a high rate of speed, the man soon lost control when he came to a curve. The next minute, his car came to an abrupt halt with two wheels in the ditch. He jumped out and ran into some bushes, shooting again as he went.

Realizing it would be foolhardy to pursue him in the dark and risk being shot when they had his car there to identify him by, they simply got the tag number and went back to check on the crowd in the street. Turned out he had indeed been shooting into the air, and no one had been hurt. It would be helpful to immediately know his name, but often the people who knew such a law-breaker would refuse to tell the police anything that might identify or incriminate the person, so learning his name from this crowd was unlikely. With this in mind, Paul told the people that the man had tragically wrecked not far down the road, not revealing that he was probably uninjured and had run away. One of the people then told Paul the man's name, thinking the family needed to be notified.

The man was brought in, charged, tried, and given 90 days in jail. The next day after the trial, Paul was in the Police Station and saw the man walk in. "What's he doing free? He was given 90 days," Paul stammered. Turned out, the man worked for the county and they needed him right now, so he was told he could start serving his time after the first of the month. Very accommodating.

Fingerprints

The FBI sent agents to the Anderson Police Department to train the policemen in matching fingerprints from suspects they arrested to those prints on file for known criminals. The photo below shows Paul studying some fingerprints.

Helen Jordan Davis, Ph.D., Th.D.

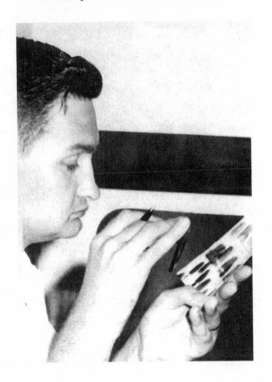

Chapter Six
Newspaper Column

Paul Jordan

"On the Beat"

Being a policeman was never just a job for Paul. He really cared about his city and the people in it. When he saw things going wrong, he wanted to fix them. What could he do? How could he have the most impact for good? He began writing a column called "On the Beat" for The Anderson Free Press newspaper, citing some of the problems he saw and offering solutions for them. He became a true crusader, particularly in his concerns for teenagers. He desperately wanted parents to be aware of the dangerous situations their teenagers were getting into and hoped the parents would intervene before the courts had to. From his vantage point, he saw things that allowed him to raise awareness of the problems for the city officials as well as the general public.

When you read the columns, if you hear the news today at all, you'll realize the concerns Paul had back then are the same concerns we have today! The columns could have been written in 2015.

For a long time he signed the columns with only his badge number, so few people knew who was writing them. Some people considered it a challenge to try and figure out who the writing cop was. The manager of the State Theater was one of those so challenged.

Every evening around 9 or 9:30 PM, the policeman who was on the square would be called to walk the theater manager to the bank with his take for the day, protecting him so he wouldn't be robbed. One night Paul was the escort. The manager began to tell Paul he was sure he had figured out who the writing policeman was. Paul just smiled to himself as the man speculated about Paul's co-workers, obviously never suspecting it was Paul. He could have simply checked Paul's badge number, but apparently he didn't realize the numbers were on the badges. Eventually the paper began to give Paul's name instead of his badge number, so the mystery was over.

When he first became a policeman, his badge number was 35. Every time someone retired, left the force for any reason, or was promoted, Paul's number moved down toward 1. By the time he left the force, his number was 3.

Frances cut out the columns and saved them in a scrapbook, some of which have survived. The columns that could be located are given in this chapter. Many have no dates, so it is impossible to know the correct order in which they were written. Where dates are known, those are given with the article. There were many more columns, written from 1964 to 1972 during his eight-and-one-half-year police career.

Letters of Support

Here is a sample of the letters received from readers of his column. This one came from Silver Spring, Maryland from a subscriber to the paper.

As a subscriber of The Anderson Free Press, although residing in the Washington, D.C. area, I find your observations relating to your general areas of interest rather interesting; and from several points of view I am personally concerned.

In your column of June 20 you implied that there are some who believe you merely sign your name to expressions of thought of others. Obviously, to me at least, your observations are interpreted as being rather candid and related to subjects of your own general interest. This pleases me, and I trust you will continue to exploit your talent for self-expression on newsworthy and interesting subjects.

Your efforts through this medium, at least, motivate some of the readers of your column to think, while stimulating others to want to think. Such, in my judgment, is what writing is all about. It is regrettable that only time will enable more people to be exposed to your thoughts.

It is with sincerity that I suggest you continue to maintain your determination to follow the dictates of your conscience and therefore share your constructive thoughts with those in your community.

Sincerely yours,
E. Buckley Hancock

In all of the columns copied here, when someone is being criticized, his or her name is omitted, even though the names were given when the original column was published.

Politics

(Dated June 20, 1968)

Before I get started on this article, allow me to explain how simple it is to write about something when you are either living it or it's existing right under your nose. I have been accused of not writing these articles—merely signing my name to them. I appreciate the compliment that it takes someone with more intelligence than myself to write these articles. I do, however, write them myself.

I just pick out a certain situation, explain what is happening, and give my opinion regarding the matter. It might not be the right opinion, but it's mine.

You can talk to people about the election of Senators and House members, and some appear not to be interested in these races. They say it doesn't matter who goes in. If they happen to have a friend who is running in one of the races, they vote for him. If not, they don't vote, period. They continuously say that this country is getting in a bad condition, but are not willing to do anything about it. Some feel one little vote doesn't count, so they don't take the time to go to the polls. They do take the time to gripe when something goes wrong, though.

It's time to do something instead of all of this complaining. Some few people have started to stir. They have looked around them, seen the condition the world is getting in, and are trying hard to do something about it.

After listening to the Republican candidates last Friday, I formed these opinions: 1) That this country truly is in a condition unpleasing to most of us, and 2) that the Democrats are now in the driver's seat and what is happening happened in their laps.

I am not saying that a person is wrong merely because he is a Democrat, or that they are right if they happen to be a Republican. What I am saying is that the Democrats, as they stand now, are way behind on everything. It appears they only want in office just to say that they are a member of the House, or whatever office they are running for. Nothing appears to be getting done. This country continues to be in a mess, and it's getting worse by the day.

I know that politics is a dirty word. I didn't like at first the way the different candidates insulted the Democrats, but I realize they were telling the truth. We have one man in the House who has only attended about 30 percent of the sessions. This man went over big in the primary election. I hope he will either be defeated or begin to show more interest in his work. How can he help us if he doesn't even think enough about the trust the people have placed in him to go to the sessions? If I am wrong, I would like to be corrected. When I found out how many sessions he had missed, my vote automatically went to the other side.

Leon Tilley stated that the roads in Anderson County were in very bad shape. To disagree with Mr. Tilley, one would have to be blind.

Donnie Ray Cooley, running for the House of Representatives, said that crime increases in the past 10 years add up to about 88 percent, while our population increase was only 10 percent. I knew that crime was increasing, but didn't have any idea that it had increased that much. He went on to say that the Supreme Court protects criminals, and you know he was right. A person doesn't really have any protection until he breaks the law. Then every legal trick is used to get him acquitted.

One out of every five persons will be attacked or affected by these criminals. It may not be a serious attack, but their hubcaps or other stuff will be stolen. The reason for this is because the law is not permitted to do anything with these criminals once they are apprehended.

Enoch Martin used the phrase "In God We Trust." He stated that this was what it was supposed to be, but the way things are going now, "In Government We Trust" is more the case. Truly the government has let us down. People wanting something for nothing, figuring that the country owes it to them, violates the meaning of government.

Take the man who robbed the bank at Spartanburg. He apparently felt that he had the right to take that which didn't belong to him. No one has the right to take that which doesn't belong to him, and certainly he doesn't have the right to take another person's life.

Frank Nixon said action should be taken regarding local and world situations, and that action is needed badly right now. I have to agree with him.

Jack Shaw discussed the faults of a judge, faults that can't and shouldn't be overlooked. He explained how he tried to tell *what had happened regarding this judge, and how he wasn't allowed by fellow legislators to speak his piece. The judge was accused of being intoxicated while in the performance of his duties—duties entrusted to him. How can a man, any man, render a just and fair verdict in such a condition?*

Why Be a Policeman?

(Dated Aug. 22, 1968)

I know readers of this column have heard people say they wouldn't be a cop in the City of Anderson or in any other city. I guess they are smart, to a certain extent. A policeman certainly can't enforce the law as necessary because of Supreme Court rulings upholding criminals.

A policeman takes a job of policing for about the same reason any man takes a job, that being to support his family, though certainly not in a stylish manner. His pay won't allow it. I firmly believe that with the shortage of policemen across the country getting worse, steps will have to be taken to make police salaries adequate.

What do I make? Just $96 a week. Can I live on that? No. My wife makes $250 a month keeping foster children to subsidize our family income.

I have hopes of a raise just like any other person of a chosen profession. I have heard it said time and time again that a man with a high school education would be crazy to take a job as a policeman. The reasons given are very sound, though I am not sold on them. One reason is a policeman might get shot trying to save somebody's life. Another is that if a criminal is arrested, more times than not he will escape punishment on some technicality.

I could name more reasons for not taking a job as a policeman than I could for taking the job. But my reasons for taking the job are good enough for me.

A soldier is drafted to fight for his country. But being a policeman is strictly an individual choice. He can quit at will. He has the satisfaction of trying to make the city in which he lives safe for his children, his wife, and loved ones. This means a lot. It doesn't make one a hero, but the job is necessary.

Sure, a lot of criminals escape punishment. A lot of drunk drivers are turned loose, and violations go unpaid. But when a drunk driver is arrested, he is temporarily taken off the road, even if he later goes free. For that moment he cannot jeopardize the lives of others.

A policeman may feel he is underpaid, but he also feels he is doing something worthwhile. There are moments of joy, moments of sorrow. He learns to accept them, not as he would like, but as he finds things. He can try to change things when he sees a better way, and sometimes he receives thanks. Sometimes he doesn't.

Discouragement comes by not doing what he would like for some people. When a mother cries over the way her husband treats her and her children, one feels like taking a stick to his hide. But he doesn't.

You ask if we need more policemen in Anderson. Certainly we do, but we can't appeal to qualified men by using a Marine Corp-type poster. One joins the Police Department because he feels the city needs him. If one wants to feel important, then police work isn't for him. If one wants to help people in various ways—and be insulted many times in the process—and perform a vital job, then apply for the job. I personally recommend it.

Helen Jordan Davis, Ph.D., Th.D.

Cop Killing

(Dated Aug. 29, 1968)

Last week, I said that if a man wanted to be important, then being a policeman wasn't for him. Allow me to apologize to the men at the Police Department. I didn't mean that statement the way I now realize it sounded. Every man certainly wants to be important. A police officer is most necessary, and he is important.

Before I get back to the importance of the Police Department, allow me to praise the new administration here in Anderson. Taking over on July 1, they were told a number of untruths by the old administration. It seems to me that men should come right out and tell each other the truth.

If the city was in a hole financially, they should have said so instead of implying there was money left over. When the new administration discovered this was very far-fetched, it affected me and every other city employee. Instead of a nice raise, we are going to have to settle for a small one.

And that audit business made every police officer look like a crook. If a man worked in the radio room and had anything to do with the handling of money, he was looked upon with suspicion. And if a man decided to go elsewhere, the public assumed he quit because he was involved in the "missing money" situation.

Certainly the previous administration should have cleared up the mess before they left office. And it would have cleared other officers if the guilty party had been pointed out. But they left it unsettled for the new administration. Happily, the new councilmen are bringing it to a head.

Allow me to express an opinion regarding an article published in The Free Press last week. I know the editor of

The Free Press would prefer to see the article entitled "Cop Killer Given the Gas Chamber." But the truth was, the only way it could read was "Cop Killer Praised."

One has to stop and ask what kind of country this is when a man, whether he is black or white, can kill an individual and receive praise for it. To me, it's a shame that a man like Black Militant Fred "Ahmed" Evans should ever even be mentioned in church and certainly should not be mentioned with praise. As for the man who praised him, he is encouraging the taking of human life.

How can a man make such a statement as the one credited to the Director of Project Head Start, a man who stupidly praised a militant for taking the lives of three policemen. He stated that he hoped that Brother Ahmed goes down in history as one of our great patriots and that he believed there were a couple of hundred more Ahmeds ready to express themselves in the great American tradition, with guns. All I can say is there must be two great American traditions. I never knew the above-mentioned way to be the American way, and I feel that any man who says so doesn't have the right to live here.

Listen to another dumb nut, the program director of the Cleveland Area Peace Action Council. He told some 100 white persons at a meeting, "You drove him to it when you dragged him from our homeland in Africa." To that man, I would say I'll give a hundred dollars or more to try to raise enough to see he gets an airplane, jet plane to be exact, back to Africa. If he feels that way about our country, I'll gladly help him get back to his.

I believe that in America a policeman tries to protect all lives, not just the lives of white people. I know here in Anderson we don't have any Negro policemen. It is not because we don't want them, but apparently they don't seem to want the job. However, when a Negro family is in trouble, *they call the Police Station and within minutes a patrol car, occupied by two white policemen, arrives and the policemen listen attentively to their problems. Then they take whatever action is necessary to straighten out the situation.*

Tomorrow Not Promised

(Dated Sept. 19, 1968)

This article is somewhat personal, but perhaps someone will find it interesting, especially if you have children of your own. We don't have children of our own yet—we're expecting our first child in December.

What I am writing about is one of our foster children, Randy, who is 14 years old. Randy has been a diabetic for over three years now. I suppose it was a hard thing for a boy of 11 to realize that he must give himself a shot of insulin every morning and then carefully watch what he eats.

The reason I'm thinking of Randy is because of a question he asked me the other night. Just out of the blue he asked, "What would you do if you only had three months to live?" I guess to say I was shocked would be putting it mildly.

I felt that I had to give an answer, and the only answer I could think of was "Do a lot of praying and be sure that I was ready to go."

Then I asked him why the question. He assured me that he was all right and that nothing was wrong. Actually, I was pretty sure he was all right physically as he had been to the doctor just a week or so before.

I guess it would be a good idea if we all lived from day to day as though we only had a few months to live.

This reminds me of something that happened several weeks ago. A close friend and I were discussing the fact that we were alive that day but had no promise of tomorrow. Today my friend is gone. I am certain that all of us could think back and remember a person who was very close to us who is now departed from this life.

On another subject: It is certainly comforting having an administration that thinks enough of the Police Department and the other departments to get out and actually work with them on problems.

The mayor and other members of the city council have started the task of cleaning up a section of Church Street. It is very commendable for them to go along with us to share the same dangers we face and to feel the satisfaction later of a job well done.

Irresponsible Parents

(Dated Oct. 3, 1968)

Maybe someone with a little more education could put more feeling into this article. It does not concern politics, but kids.

About a week ago Patrolman George Smith and I were riding together. We stopped to check out one of the beer joints and saw a sight that displeased both of us. In the first booth sat a man and a woman drinking beer. With them was a son about four years old. We thought of making a case against them for contributing to the delinquency of a minor, but realized they probably could prove the child was too young to know what they were doing. The couple said they would gladly leave, so we let them go.

Thinking back, I realized it is families like this one that one day will be separated, and the children will be the ones hurt the most. I realized there are hundreds of kids right here in Anderson County who never really had a chance at home, kids who have had nothing but one disappointment after another.

Perhaps one day that second chance will come, but it will hurt because that's when they are taken from their parents and placed in foster homes. Usually, no matter how much they have been hurt or the times they have had to go without, they still love their parents. It hurts when they are removed. Finally, though, they get adjusted to the foster homes. The man and wife keeping them become a mother and dad and try to raise them right. Foster parents try to give the children everything they think they need.

Last week the Anderson Fair came along. The Association, or some of the Fair officials, promised foster children a big day. This day was to be on Monday, and the children were promised they could ride until their hearts were content, and they could eat.

Foster parents arranged for the children to either stay out of school or get out early for the special day at the Fair. The Welfare Office told them to be at the Fair around 1 P.M. Mr. Boozer and several case workers came to the Fairground thinking the ride operators had been told and were prepared for the children's arrival. Instead, sadly, the operators were uncooperative.

Around five o'clock, hours after arrival, the kids had ridden only two rides and a lot of them were hungry. When I got there, I asked if they were having a good time and was told of the course of events that had taken place. Mr. Boozer asked me to help. I went to Mr. I.V. Hume's office. Mrs. Hume said he was out, but she sent a representative of the Chamber of Commerce to explain to the ride operators that the foster children had been promised a day at the Fair.

After one ride, the kids were starving, so we went to the refreshment stand. The kids were given one hot dog and nothing to drink. Finally, they received a drink.

At 8:30 P.M. I saw Mr. Boozer again, and he said the situation wasn't much better, and some of the kids had gone home. Mr. Boozer got permission from the mayor and Capt. Walt Embler for me to accompany the group. At this point it was about 9 o'clock, but the remaining 16 kids got to ride most of the rides.

We were confronted by another problem at midnight. There was no transportation. Mr. Boozer was the only Welfare worker left, and I didn't have my car. Most of the patrol cars had left, but there was the Police Paddy Wagon. This served as the mode of transportation to take the children home.

In closing, I want to say that I don't believe what happened would have come about had Mr. and Mrs. Hume been aware of the situation. I know them personally and think a lot of them

Next year I am going to try to arrange to spend the day with the children. I feel they have been disappointed enough for a lifetime.

Judgment Against a Law Officer

(Dated Oct. 10, 1968)

I would like to express this article in a dramatic way. By dramatic I mean in a way so you, the reader, will feel as though it definitely concerns not only me but everyone in the state, especially the citizens of Anderson County.

I know most of you are familiar with the recent Supreme Court decisions regarding the law. Most of us have in recent weeks read in the newspapers where a man, more specifically a lawbreaker, has gone free because of some loophole in the law. This hasn't been just in cases where minor violations have occurred, but in serious violations such as murder.

The Supreme Court has managed to make law enforcement officers almost afraid to enforce the law. An officer has to be extremely careful in making a case. If he leaves any strings untied, the lawbreaker is quick to take advantage of him. He is a man who takes his profession seriously, but there is something he must take more seriously, and that is the welfare of his family. When a law enforcement officer is sued, that affects his family.

In the surrounding countryside there are little plaques reading, "Support your law enforcement." Most people do support the law. Let us remember that a policeman or a deputy, any law official, is only a man. He is not perfect by any means. He doesn't have a law degree. He tries to enforce the law in a manner that he thinks is fair to all parties concerned.

Imagine if you will, going on vacation and returning to your home. Something doesn't seem quite right. You're just a little leery about going into your house. What do you do? Call either the Sherriff's Department or the Police Department. Within minutes several law enforcement officers arrive and check your house to make sure everything is all right.

I hope this doesn't sound like some 10-cent novel. I don't mean that the policeman might happen to be a hero, because 99 times out of 100 no one is in the house. You don't have to take the chance. A law officer can be reached day or night. I would like to think he is a dedicated man, dedicated to enforcing the law, safe-guarding the people, and assisting in any way possible.

I believe you are backing us up 100 percent. Based upon this belief and my faith in the citizens of Anderson County, I am asking for your help. As you know, recent Supreme Court rulings against a local law enforcement officer resulted in a $10,000 judgment against him, which he must satisfy personally.

Most law officers are bonded. They are expected to perform their duties as law enforcement officers, but if they make a mistake and the bonding company is in any way involved, they look to that officer to personally make restitution, even to the point of getting a judgment against what a man owns.

Decide for yourself whether you think a law officer should be treated in this manner. If you feel this is wrong, as I do, send any contribution to the Defense Fund. By giving your support, no matter how large or small, you will be supporting the law.

Time For a Change

(Dated Oct. 17, 1968)

In April of this year the people of Anderson elected a Republican mayor and seven Republican aldermen. Only one Democrat was elected. Notable changes have resulted, even at this point.

Acting upon a request from the people, the Police Department formed a special squad to clean up Church Street. The results have been good. To show the police they are supported, the mayor and several aldermen went to Church Street with the policemen. The mayor still works quite a bit with the police.

What kind of fellow is our mayor? To know him is to like him. He will joke with you, and he can get serious. He is a man you can talk to, reason with, and I firmly believe that the whole administration has the interest of the people at heart.

The city manager is a business-type person, but also one you can talk to. He will listen to any complaints. Already he has suggested plans to improve the city's efficiency. He has implemented plans which give the employees better working conditions and a little more money.

In about a month there will be another election, this one for county and state posts and, more importantly, a presidential election. As far as the state and county elections are concerned, I support the Republican Party 100 percent. I believe that most of the Republican candidates will be elected. I attended one Democrat meeting, and all the candidates of this party seem to say they would continue to give the same type government they have given in the past. To me, that's not a good type of government. The Republicans ask, "Are you ready for a change?" I say, "Yes, I am." I know the Republicans have plans that will help our county grow.

Blackie Wynn

(Dated Oct. 24, 1968)

On Sunday night, Officer George Smith and I received a call about a party on P & N Court. At his own request, we are using his name in this story.

On Sunday night, he was at the end of his road. He told us how his wife had left him, and that he had lost his children because the courts felt he couldn't take proper care of them. With one side completely paralyzed, a diabetic and an epileptic, he hoped he could die. We tried to reassure him that there is always something to live for.

He became calmer, but still was deeply hurt by the fact that everyone seemed to have forgotten him.

Later when I mentioned his name, some of the older policemen remembered when he was a prize fighter in splendid physical condition. I feel he is better qualified to tell his own story. So, let me introduce Charles "Blackie" Wynn.

"I started in sports at the age of 14, playing football. I won the Silver Gloves and later the Golden Gloves in boxing. After the war began, I was middleweight champ at Fort Bragg, N.C., then went on to become champ of the 8th Army in the Pacific by knocking out Tony Maronino in two rounds. Later it took Sugar Ray Robinson eight rounds to knock Tony out.

"In football, we had a good team here, and I made all-state and played in the Shrine Bowl for crippled children. I have taken part in sports for the Heart Fund and the Cancer Fund, and I am proud of the trophies I won during my years in sports. All that remains are the trophies and scrapbooks, for I suffered a crippling stroke. But thanks to these policemen, I have found something better. I have turned to the Lord, and He is everything."

Blackie would appreciate your prayers, and asks that you hold fast to your memories of him. For those of you who saw him in an exhibition with Charlie Thompson, that won't be hard to do.

Turning to another subject, let me tell you about a new restaurant in town serving delicious food and open 24 hours a day. Don't be surprised if you see policemen, highway patrolmen, or other law enforcement officers eating at Carlos'.

A strong supporter of the law, Carlos allows us to eat half-price, giving us about our only chance of getting a good steak. I am a good-sized man with an appetite to match, but I couldn't quite eat all he put on my plate, and it was really good.

Good luck to Blackie Wynn and thanks to Carlos. See you next week.

Don't Just Stand By

(No date)

Suppose you were trying to sell the idea that America is the best country to live in. How would you sell a person on this idea if the person has the capability to check everything you said? What excuses would you make for all the senseless killings we have in this country? Would you try to ignore the question by saying there are some good Americans and some bad ones?

What about the problems we are having with our teenagers? Would you say they are just kids and let them have their fun? How about 13 and 14-year-olds drinking beer? Would you just simply deny this, say that it does not happen? Or, if you admitted it did happen, would you say it merely pertains to somebody else's kids, not yours?

What about the riots and civil disorders in this country? Would you say it's not you but somebody else? What about these "adult only" movies and trashy magazines before us and our youth? Would you say you don't go to this type of movie or read this type of magazine, and your kids don't either—you think?

What explanation would you give when asked about taking the Bible out of schools? Would you say that was somebody else's doings, not yours? How about the young boy who got so disgusted with life he killed himself? Would you just say it wasn't in your neighborhood and it certainly wasn't your boy? What about the two adults who killed each other after arguing over a dish of ice cream? Would you say you haven't argued over anything as foolish as that, and you certainly haven't killed anyone?

How about the two boys who played Russian roulette with a double-barreled shotgun? Or the four boys who just the other night, while looking for "kicks," passed by a supermarket and stole bread and pies left earlier by a bread truck? What these boys didn't steal, they scattered all over the place. When they were unsuccessful in selling some of the items they took, they became angry and threw a bottle through a plate-glass window of a business. These boys, by the way, were drinking heavily.

Then there was the boy who had just turned 14 and was given a car on his birthday. Less than a week later he was killed after betting he could make a curve at 70 miles an hour—while the posted speed limit was 15 miles an hour.

Sometimes just being an innocent bystander to such things as I have enumerated here—all of which are true— isn't enough. We must take a bigger stand: stop denying, stop running away, stand firm. Let neither hell nor high water stop us from doing that which we know to be right.

Juvenile Delinquency

(Dated Oct. 31, 1968)

I know by now that almost everyone has heard about the incident at the YMCA parking lot on Oct. 18, but allow me to give a brief run-down on what took place.

71

At about nine o'clock that night a patrol car occupied by Mayor Richard Otter, Patrolmen Billy Newton, Hershel Childs, George Smith, and myself went to the Y parking lot to check out a complaint about teenagers drinking beer and engaging in other types of unpleasing behavior.

We parked the patrol car next to the Y and slipped unobserved to the parking lot. First we saw several boys standing around a car. As we closed in on the car, one youth, who was only 14 years old, tried to hide a can of beer. A closer look revealed two cases of beer in the car. The driver was 16 years old.

There were beer cans and bottles scattered over the parking lot. We estimated that between 25 and 30 youths could have been caught red-handed had we had enough men to block the exits from the parking lot.

The car containing the two cases of beer was the first car we came upon. Less than an hour later several more youths were apprehended with beer, liquor, and glue, used for sniffing. This time State Agents Bob White and Bill Tidwell caught the teenagers.

Mr. White said he could reveal things about teenagers drinking that would make anyone sick. We are all concerned about the monkeys who sell these youths beer and whiskey. If the parents of these kids feel strongly about it, as I am sure they must, then perhaps they could encourage their kids to reveal the source from which they purchase alcoholic beverages.

I don't advocate closing the Y because this incident occurred outside, and Y personnel cannot check cars on the outside and supervise the young people on the inside. Parents certainly should be informed of what is going on, and by doing so, perhaps the parking lot will become less of a problem.

There really are not many places a teenager can go in Anderson, but this is no excuse for some of the conduct that goes on. In my opinion, much of this conduct originates from a general belief that the local juvenile authority will be "soft" on them if they are caught.

For example, an angry father contacted me last week about his son who a few weeks ago was involved with other youths in damaging bread and cakes unloaded in front of a supermarket. These youths also threw a bottle through a plate glass window, and took the breather off of a car.

This man's son was sentenced to pay a fine of $12.50 and was placed on probation. A short time thereafter he was again caught involved in a crime, was brought before the same juvenile authority, and again given a suspended sentence. If he's caught again, he'll be given another suspended sentence.

I believe there is a time to be tough and a time to be gentle. Presently, toughness is needed. The lack of toughness by our juvenile setup is evidenced by the fact that a large portion of the court's business involves repeat offenders.

A change is desperately needed.

A news article in the paper the next day, after the night Paul wrote about, described the situation in more detail, stating that 11 boys ages 14, 15, and 16 were arrested for possession of alcoholic beverages and glue-sniffing material. The occupants of only four cars were apprehended, while it was estimated that at least a third of the occupants of the 30 to 40 cars were youths illegally drinking beer and whiskey. This news article described the situation as being just as dire as Paul had stated.

In response to Paul's article a seven-member panel was convened to discuss this issue at the McDuffie Parent Teacher Student Association meeting on Nov. 23rd, approximately one month later. Paul was the Moderator of the panel, which consisted of: State Sen. Ed Garrison,

Judge Harry Agnew, Harry Findley, an Anderson banker, Rev. Wesley Strong, Minister of Education at St. John's Methodist Church, Mrs. Boyce Glenn, Jr., a mother and worker with young people, and Lynn Shiflet, a senior at McDuffie School.

No concrete plans were made, but the issue was thoroughly discussed. Paul's article had raised awareness of this problem to a new level.

Concerns For Children

(Dated Nov. 14, 1968)

Not long ago I wrote about Charles "Blackie" Wynn. He is still not doing well and probably will be in the Veterans Hospital at Augusta, Ga. for a while. He would appreciate cards and letters from the folks back home.

While driving along North Street recently, I noticed a little boy and girl, about ages two and three, who appeared to be lost. I stopped and tried to talk to them. Neither could be sure where their home was or anything. Several people passing by offered their help, including Mr. and Mrs. Bill Darby. I appreciate the help all these people gave me. The mother of the children found us about a half hour later. She was grateful for our efforts and promised she would watch the children closer.

Here's a new one. A 14-year-old boy was detected at a theater last week sniffing dry cleaning fluid. Wendell Patterson, the theater manager, called the Police Department to report the incident. I answered the call. The manager was concerned, and I don't believe he wanted the boy punished. He just wanted him to realize the harm he was doing to himself.

To Mr. Patterson I say thanks. If everyone would do as he did, perhaps we could bring a halt to glue sniffing, beer drinking, and other unpleasing behavior by our teenagers.

The other night Patrolmen Billy Newton, Charles Broome, and Charles Partain brought into the police station a boy so drunk he didn't know where he was. The boy's parents were contacted, but apparently they couldn't do much with him for the next night he was among a group of boys drinking in a car chased by Patrolman Jack Brown. The boy resisted arrest and tried to get away. A local doctor was in the vicinity and lent assistance to the patrolman.

In contrast to that episode, I recently had the privilege of showing a group of Boy Scouts around the jail. It was nice seeing such well-behaved youngsters. You could see in these boys the character molded by Boy Scout training. Our community owes a great debt to those adults who devote their time to carrying out the Boy Scout program.

This is personal but something I wish to share with you. It concerns one of my foster children. Parents of foster children have to keep in mind the fact that some day they may have to give up the children.

Today, Thursday, a boy who has been in my family for three years will appear in family court and probably be returned to his mother. We think the world of this boy, who is a diabetic, but we feel he belongs with his mother. The mother's only fault, as far as my wife and I could see, was that she loved the boy too much. She had pity on him because of his condition and as a result of this pity, she got him almost everything he wanted. At least, she got him everything he wanted that she could afford.

The boy's system wasn't as strong as his desire to have some things. As a result, he became very sick. We feel now that his mother will be more strict with him, and we wish both of them all the luck in the world.

When Paul was patrolling in the evening, he would see many teenagers gathered in the parking lot of Belvedere Plaza. When he drew close enough, he could see the whiskey bottles, but by the time he could park and get out of the patrol car, the kids would have set the bottles down. When a bottle was between two teenagers, he would ask to whom it belonged. They each would deny it was his, so Paul would just reach and get it, saying, "Well, since nobody knows whose it is, let's just pour it out." Then he would pour it out on the pavement. He knew they could go get more from the place they had gotten that bottle, but it would delay them for a while and deter them somewhat because of the expense. He was always concerned for their safety, especially drinking and driving.

City Code

(Dated Nov. 21, 1968)

By now almost everyone knows of the untimely death last week of Charles "Blackie" Wynn. Blackie seemed to be doing fine at the Veterans Hospital where he was a patient, and was actually preparing to come home in a few days. I would like to extend to his friends and relatives my heartfelt sympathy in their loss.

Last week I wrote about a teenager getting arrested for drunkenness on a Friday night, then again on a Saturday night. Parents are morally and legally responsible for the action of their children, and there is a section in the City Code which reads: "Whenever any person who is a minor and who has been arrested and convicted in the municipal court for disorderly conduct, is unable to pay the fine imposed upon him, it shall be the duty of the Chief of Police to send by one of the policemen a written notice to the parents or guardian of such minor, notifying such parent or guardian that if such minor is again convicted before such court, such parent or guardian will be deemed guilty of a misdemeanor. When any parent or guardian shall have received such notice and shall thereafter permit such child or ward to go at large in the streets, and such child shall be convicted a second or any subsequent time in such court of disorderly behavior in the streets, such parents or guardians shall be deemed guilty of a misdemeanor. Provided that such parents or guardians shall first have due notice to appear before such court and show cause, if any, why he should not be punished." End of quote!

I hope my previous article about the Y will do more good than harm. I feel that teenagers should have a place to socialize, but in the right manner. By socializing I certainly don't mean drinking or conducting themselves in a manner unfit to be seen in public.

Mr. Sellers at "The Court of Swing" called me and stated that he agreed with my ideas concerning teenagers 100 percent. He told me that "The Court of Swing" has definite rules and they stick to them because of their interest in teenagers. I have never been there but will check it out soon. It would be a good idea for parents to attend the first night with their youngsters to get a good idea whether or not the place is suitable for their children. At least give the kids a chance.

Teen Recreation Panel

(No date)

On Thursday (Nov. 23, 1968) I had the rare opportunity of attending a PTA meeting at McDuffie High School. I really enjoyed it and learned quite a lot. Mrs. Dean Hall, Program Chairman, allowed me to serve as Moderator on a panel which discussed teenagers. There are others far better qualified than myself, but I really appreciated the honor.

One of the main questions asked was: "Do Teenagers Have the Proper Recreation?" I came to the meeting completely unprepared, not realizing it was a PTA meeting. However, what I had to say was my own opinion and really didn't need to be rehearsed.

I made one mistake, which the Rev. Wesley Strong corrected me on. I agreed with him 100 percent. I'm talking about teenagers drinking and sniffing glue.

What I said was that teenagers would drink if you took them to the Y.M.C.A or if you took them to church. I said the Y was just a building and the church was just a building, and I meant that if they had the opportunity and the inclination, they would drink anywhere. What happened on the Y parking lot has also happened on a church parking lot.

But Rev. Strong said the church isn't just a building, that it is the Lord's house and should be referred to as such. I have always believed in treating it that way. What I should have said was the Y.M.C.A. or the church was just a meeting place to these youngsters. It apparently makes little difference to them where they are, and they have the beer and whiskey with them.

Judge Agnew brought out an interesting fact. He stated that 95 percent of the crimes committed were by persons under 28 years of age.

Lynn Schiflet said there are only a few places teenagers can go. She stated that the only types of movies being shown are suggested for mature audiences and are lacking in decency. I agree and would like to see Anderson have an old-timey movie theater, showing only those pictures approved by a specially appointed group from different churches. I can remember back 10 years ago (or was it further back than that?) that kids could go to a movie, and you didn't worry about it. I used to enjoy a decent movie now and then.

I am 100 percent FOR the teenagers. I disapprove strongly of the activities some of them indulge in. There are good teenagers, and we should do all we can to keep them that way. We should also try to help those who have gone astray.

I can't actually print in the newspaper some of the things that go on right now, but I would be happy to reveal the facts to anyone who will listen to me.

Support the Y

(No date)

Every story has two sides, and I hate to always be looking on the bad side. Thus, when I wrote last week about teenagers drinking on the YMCA parking lot, it was not my intention to have the Y closed.

I think the socials held at the Y on Friday nights should continue, but they should be chaperoned better. I would suggest that a committee of parents be formed. With 15 or 20 parents chaperoning on the inside, and keeping a close watch on the parking lot as well, the socials would fill the need for which they were designed.

I wish every parent could go at least once to the Y and get an idea of what teenagers enjoy. A visit by parents would enable them to contribute suggestions on how to make the events more enjoyable.

For anyone to say the Y is a bad place is very foolish. It's only a building. People make it good or bad. What happened on the Y parking lot has happened on a church parking lot.

Kids need guidance. We shouldn't do away with their fun, but adults should recognize their responsibility to teach their children the right kind of fun.

What occurred on the Y parking lot didn't hurt the kids on the wrong side of the tracks, so to speak. It hurt the good kids—the kids whose parents were shocked at what happened and as a result, they forbade their kids to go back.

The kids on the wrong side of the track will drink anyway, even if they have to find another place to park.

I believe we owe it to our kids to take them to the Y and make them aware that no good time is derived from drinking or participating in other vices that include unpleasing behavior.

Anderson teenagers need a place to go. Today's movies, for the most part, are trash. The Y certainly is a decent place for children of all ages to participate in various forms of activity.

Youngsters seem to be foremost in my thoughts. Every time I arrest a father or mother for being drunk, I think about how it affects their children. I try to console myself by saying I didn't provide the parents with whiskey. I didn't cause them to fight. They broke the law, and I, as a police officer, had a duty to perform.

Neither do the children contribute to the conditions or conduct of their parents. This brings to my mind a recent incident where a mother and father of eight children were involved in a wreck on Reed St. The man was so drunk he couldn't stand up, and his wife was drinking. I had no choice but to arrest the man.

Another case coming to my mind involved a man who got so drunk he pulled out a pistol and declared that he was going to shoot someone. During his shooting spree, a bullet struck a 12-year-old girl on the top of the head. Luckily she wasn't seriously hurt, but had the bullet struck an inch lower, she would have been instantly killed.

In closing, I offer thanks to Mr. Waldrep of B St. for sending me a letter. I enjoyed his comments and invite other readers to relay their thoughts on various situations to me. I have an open mind. If anyone shows me that I am wrong in some of my observations, I will admit it.

Questions Answered

(No date)

This week I shall attempt to answer questions ranging from why I write this column to what is a drunk.

I guess there are several reasons why I write. Maybe these reasons will not suit some people, but they are good enough for me. To begin with, I enjoy expressing my opinions. Second, though it makes me sound self-centered, it makes me feel good to see my name in print, something I've never denied. Third, and most importantly, I see the same problems cropping up over and over, and I feel the public needs to be aware of them. We need to get involved and change things for the better.

No, I don't get paid for writing. I never have thought that my columns were composed in a manner that merits pay. I have received a number of compliments, which I will always treasure. These include letters, telephone calls, and comments from people on the street.

My involvement in politics has been nothing but my opinions based on what I knew to be the truth or based on what I believed to be the truth.

As I have stated, the above reasons may not be good enough for some people, but to me they are sufficient.

What kind of atmosphere is there when I write, or just when do I write, some may ask. I usually write while sitting by the television. It is 1:30 P.M. as I write this. The Mike

Douglas show is on TV. My wife just left to go to the doctor. We are expecting the stork in about two weeks. See, I just got off on another subject.

Now on the question of what is a drunk, I have no doctor's degree, so my answer will be only an opinion. The circumstances under which I would arrest one for drunkenness involve the answers to these questions: Is the person in such a condition that he cannot take care of himself? Is the person causing trouble? Is the person capable of getting home safely, or would I be endangering his life or someone else's life by allowing him to go home?

I know that commenting on drunks seems as though I have run out of something to write about. So, I will close with a joke.

There was this fellow who was being tried for public drunkenness, and the judge asked, "What brings you here?" The drunk replied, "Two polices." "Drunk, I presume?" the judge asked. "Yes, your Honor, both of them!" said the defendant.

See, I have a sense of humor, also.

The Right Leader

(No date)

I don't care who says, "Let's get the Bible back into our school system." I merely appreciate it being said. I don't care who says, "Give the law back to the people," just as long as the law does go back to the people.

I mean it doesn't matter if the person running for office and says these things is a Democrat, Republican, or Independent. If a man feels that the rights of the people come first and wants to give the law back to the people, he has my vote. Usually he will have sound reasoning behind his thinking and an idea about how to do this.

If the man who is the head of our country can somehow see that these things are carried out, then certainly this man's every decision concerning the welfare of our schools, our homes, our jobs, must be important to us. Let us vote for the candidate and this platform, not the party just because we've always voted for that party.

When it comes to something that is going to concern my way of life, I should vote for the person most qualified and not for a friend or the man who simply has a certain party label. The man and his platform are important.

Admonishment

(Dated Dec. 5, 1968)

A week ago the Police Department received a report that someone had fired a shotgun at an establishment in the 1500 block of N. Main St. Within minutes several policemen were at the scene. A crowd of youngsters pointed toward a lumberyard and yelled repeatedly, "He went that way!"

Investigation disclosed, however, that the one who did the shooting was probably in the crowd of people standing around. Apparently one boy, whom I shall refer to as Donnie, was having the time of his life.

It makes one sick to think that those watching the incident must have thought Donnie was a big man at the time of the shooting. No one would talk. Later Donnie bragged about what he had done—and gotten away with.

I ask this of Donnie: Now that everything is over, now that you've gotten away with it, do you really feel like a man? I feel sorry for anyone who has to get his "kicks" in such a manner, knowing that someone could not only get hurt but killed.

A gun is a tool. It was made for a useful purpose. To use it as a toy or to use it foolishly is, in my opinion, very unwise and childish. Grow up, Donnie. You are only belittling yourself. But I don't expect you to own up to the incident. In dealings with you in the past, you were everything but a man. I merely hope you will see the error of your way before it's too late.

What happened at a service station on N. Main St. later is an example of what can happen when a person uses a gun foolishly. Those two boys who got shot could be a lot worse off. You know the details, Donnie.

I maintain that it takes far more guts to stand up for what is right than it does to "go along with the crowd." A Christian is no weakling.

On the matter of drinking, I wish I could say something that would hit home. I hate to always be referring to the conduct of the offspring of one of our elected officials. The other night I met another one of his sons. He was drinking pretty heavily and figured he could order food in a downtown café, change the order two or three times, waiting each time until the cook had prepared the food.

Finally, when the price turned out to be 30 cents more than he figured, the boy told the cook to forget the order. He said he didn't want the food and refused to pay for it. When the management said he would call the police, the boy still refused to pay. When the police arrived, he still refused to pay.

When the boy was asked about his drinking, he admitted he was and said there was nothing wrong with drinking. How a boy can be so misguided is beyond me.

Judge Ness is due commendation for the way he handled a juvenile. A boy was given probation, but only after he serves ample time. Perhaps if the sentence is rough enough, there won't be a second time. I hate to see anyone punished, but I had rather see a youngster serve time now than see him later receive a death sentence or life imprisonment.

To the one who asked me about Richard Petty, I guess anyone can switch horses. Perhaps he feels a Ford is better.

Typical Shift?

(Dated Dec. 31, 1968)

No eight-hour period is ever the same for policemen. Two men can sometimes ride for eight hours and not receive a single call. Then they may get 10 or 15 calls in one night.

The radio operator is the one who has a rough time on those busy nights. He has to answer the telephone, check on prisoners, book prisoners, and contact patrolmen. Ben Turner is one of the radio operators who has had several years' experience in this type work, although he has only been with the city a short time.

When there is trouble, it's up to Ben to get all the information about what has happened, then decide whether officers are needed on the scene. Then it's KDV 437 to car 17 or 15 or 10 or 13 or whatever car is closer to the action.

A prowler requires fast action, and he must send the closest car. An automobile accident calls for one of the traffic men.

There are many things to think about when you are patrolling. A police officer can be riding along slowly, then suddenly the radio operator advises a burglar alarm is going off at a specified location. All units head in that direction, and the place is completely surrounded in a matter of minutes. The owner or manager is called to open the door. Some officers go in, others stay at all exits in case someone tries to escape.

Quite often the burglar is surprised at the scene of the crime, especially now that there are more patrolmen.

Break-ins are decreasing also now that there are extra cars. A burglar has no way of knowing just where the police are.

To give you an idea of a typical eight-hour period, on one long sheet of one 4 P.M. to 12 Midnight shift, there were seven calls for officers, one of which needed an assist. They included runs to check on teenagers in trouble, drunken drivers, plain drunkenness, family trouble, a fight, more teenagers in trouble, and assault and battery. It keeps everyone hopping: Captain Walter Embler, Lt. Louie Brock, and all the other officers.

A personal note as something so wonderful has happened, I can't wait to tell it. On Dec. 28 at 8:20 A.M., my wife presented me with a 7 lb. 12 ounce daughter, Kimberly Ann, our first. When the nurse told me those precious words, "Mother and daughter doing fine," it was such good news. God give me the wisdom to raise her right and help me remember to "train up a child in the way it should go, and when it is old, it will not depart from it."

Criticism of Christ

(Dated Jan. 9, 1969)

In the past I have written about many things, including a judge, teenagers, and politics, but now I have a subject that I feel is more important than any of these. This is about a man's opinion.

I believe that anyone has the right to express his or her opinion, and that anyone also has a right to take exception to that opinion.

I am referring to the person who wrote a letter to the editor in last week's edition. He told of reading an interesting editorial in the Dec. 12th edition about a leftist magazine, "The Presbyterian Survey."

In his letter, he called Jesus a rabble rouser and an agitator. Apparently he read some Scripture and interpreted it to please himself. I read his letter several times to make sure I wasn't reading it wrong.

At first I thought he could not be a church-goer, but in reading the last paragraph, I gathered he did go to church. He said, "If we conservatives intend to keep these things from happening in our church and in our city, we will have to do what the church in His day did. We will have to destroy by words or acts all of those who would follow this Christ and disrupt our good conservative way of life."

How can there be a church without Christ? Christ is the Head of the Church. To me, going to church is a form of education, a way to learn more about a man who loved us enough to die for us.

There cannot be a Bible that teaches that Christ was wrong, that He caused trouble. We must not destroy the wonderful things He taught us.

Christ was man enough to love His enemies and do good to them that hated Him. He left a perfect mark, and it's a shame to Christianity when someone distorts His teachings to suit his own fancy.

Even those who are lost most likely know that Christ's way is the right way. He would not tell us to destroy but to love.

America's Principles

(No date)

Listening to a record in which a man was writing a letter to his teenage son, I found this man's reasoning very sound.

"*Dear Son,*" the father starts, "*you ask my reaction to long hair or beards on young people. Some great men have worn long hair and beards, such as George Washington and Abraham Lincoln. If to you long hair and beards are a symbol of independence, if you believe in your heart that the principles of this country and our heritage are worthy of this display of pride that all men shall remain free, that free men at all times will not inflict their personal limitations of achievement on others, demand your own rights as well as the rights of others and be willing to fight for that right, you have my blessing. You ask that I not judge you merely as a teenager but to judge you on your own personal habits, abilities, and goals. This is a fair request, and I promise that I will not judge any person only as a teenager.*

"*You ask me if God is dead. This is a question each individual must answer within himself. Could a warm summer day with all its brightness and all its sound just happen? Just remember that God is a Guide and not a Storm Trooper. You must realize that many of the past and present generation, because of a good intention and misconceptions, have attempted to legislate morality. This has created a need for your generation to rebel against society. With this knowledge, perhaps your children will never ask if God is dead. I sometimes think much of mankind is attempting to work Him to death.*

"You ask my opinion of Draft-card burners. I would answer this way. All past wars have been dirty, unfair, immoral, and bloody. However, history has shown that most of them were necessary. If you doubt that our free enterprise system in the U.S. is worth protecting, if you doubt that the principles upon which this country was founded, that we remain free to choose our religion, our individual endeavor and our method of government, then it's doubtful if you belong here."

****

I certainly hope that none of my kids will ever have to ask if God is dead. Certainly we all see evidence of His being alive, and this country is worth fighting for, although it needs drastic changes in some parts of the government.

A final note regarding the Police Department. Last Saturday night, Mayor Richard Otter and Aldermen Norman Wham and Charles Crowe were present at the Police Station and saw how unruly one of our younger citizens could act. A young man was arrested for leaving the scene of an accident, reckless driving, loud swearing, and disorderly conduct. This boy was only 18 years old. He seemed to hate the police with a passion.

Later that night when his folks came for him, this boy tried to tell his mother a number of untruths about what had happened to him. His mother replied, "We know, Son, how crooked they are." His sister, in her twenties, said, "We will get a lawyer for you Monday." The boy's father told them both to shut up. Later that very night the sister called the police to come to a beer joint where she was having trouble with her husband. When Officer Harold Huff and I arrived, she was arguing with her husband while holding a six-month-old baby. The baby was wet with beer, which her husband had poured on her and the baby. Lt. Harrison Poore joined us and we finally quieted them down and left. About half an hour later we received a call from the mother stating that her son-in-law was threatening to kill all of them. It made me wonder. If we were so crooked as she had stated, why did they keep calling us to straighten out their family difficulties?

Well, I guess that is the life of a policeman: cussed when you do, and cussed when you don't. And I still like the job.

Family Troubles

(Dated Jan. 30, 1969)

I have written several articles concerning teenagers, and I have been told there is no need for such alarm about them. It was said they are no different now than they were years ago, and they drank and smoked then.

To me, it seems that more things are out in the open and that they drink now with a sense of pride instead of a sense of guilt and shame. Someone asks, "What is wrong with drinking beer? Or whiskey?"

This will never be an accepted thing with me. The other night, three teenagers received permission to spend the night with a friend. About 4 A.M., they were picked up at a café, drinking. One of the boys actually passed out. He had to be carried from a vehicle to the police car and then to City Hall. He was later turned over to a grateful father, who seemed very surprised to see his son in such a condition. The other two fathers also assured us that proper corrective measures would be administered.

In the past few months, there have been several cases involving both boys and girls, where the parents believed their children were spending the night at a friend's home.

They were horrified and shocked to find their children at the Police Station involved in trouble in some form. It would be so simple to make a phone call and know for sure that their son or daughter was really where they were supposed to be. I would rather show what the teenagers call "distrust" and prevent them from getting involved in something that might affect them for the rest of their lives.

Kids are youngsters for just a short period of time. I would rather mine grow up having "no fun" than not grow up at all. I know that raising a teenager is a problem, and it's easier to let them do as they please, but if we really love them, we will use discipline to make them mind and always encourage them in the right way.

Another thing parents and adults can do is to set the right example. What else can you expect if you don't? One night Officer Harold Huff and I received a call to investigate a signal 9, "family trouble." Our investigation revealed that a man and his wife were having a fight in the presence of their children. The father had been drinking.

We attempted to discuss the problem with both parties and tried to reach some kind of agreement. The mother demanded that we lock up her husband. We had no warrant, and he had not broken the law in our presence, so we could not lock him up.

Without waiting for this explanation, the man pulled off his coat and told us we might take him in, but we would surely know he didn't want to go. He said we would have to use our black-jacks on him to take him in. The kids started screaming and crying then. The man's father was present and was as white as a sheet. Officer Huff had known the man from boyhood, and he finally managed to talk him down, telling him we would take him if we had to, but we would rather he just calm down.

Looking back, it's hard to know just what the man hoped to gain by fighting with his wife, resisting arrest, and frightening his father and children.

Part of a policeman's job is to try and straighten out trouble like this. Thank goodness, all parents aren't like this.

The boy and girl I have been writing about went to family court with their mother and stepfather there. They had a lawyer, which I felt wasn't really necessary, as neither appeared to want the children. The boy and girl were turned over to the Welfare Office to be placed in a foster home, which neither parent protested. They appeared perfectly satisfied with the court's decision.

As for the boys telling their parents they were staying with a friend while actually they were out drinking at 4 A.M., Friday night a 14-year-old told his folks he was going to a social. We picked him up when a downtown neighbor reported a prowler on her back porch. Three other boys ran, and we took the 14-year-old home, hoping his parents would take care of the situation. They thanked us for going to this trouble. Later the same night, four boys were arrested, and they had about six half-pints of whiskey. They were older, and I couldn't help thinking that perhaps they started just like that 14-year-old, who has well-to-do parents.

The other night we were called to a home where a 19-year-old daughter was drunk, and the mother was using profanity with every other word while screaming for us to get the daughter out of the house. The daughter was blaming the mother for the trouble, and each was threatening to kill the other. It seemed to me that both of them could use a little old-fashioned church-going.

Life Decisions

(Dated Feb. 13, 1969)

Having written so much about the bad side of teenagers, I have a feeling I have overlooked the good side, and there certainly is a good side.

I guess I will always be writing about kids in some form. It's hard to say why I'm interested in kids or why I feel it's so important for them to go straight. I am no saint, certainly.

My thoughts turn back to the year I was in second grade attending Cleo Baily Grammar School. I remember quite well Mrs. Bolt, my teacher, arriving at school one morning. I just had to tell the teacher something. I had gotten saved the night before at a revival meeting conducted by J. Harold Smith. It was a big moment for me, and realizing this, the teacher allowed me to tell the class about it. Of course, there was much I didn't know at this early age, but I did know I was supposed to try real hard to live right.

As I grew up, my mother always had us at church. She didn't send us, either, she stayed with us. We were there for Sunday School, preaching, Training Union, and preaching again. Then just as sure as Wednesday night came, we were back at church. My mother was my Junior Class teacher at church, and my father taught a class, too.

It was when I was in the fourth grade that I decided I wanted to be a preacher. Every morning just before leaving for school, Daddy would sit us all down and let me read some verses from the Bible. I wanted to be a preacher until I was nearly 16. Then I became swayed between two choices. One was to be a preacher, the other to be a policeman.

I never was certain if the Lord wanted me to be a preacher, and I felt that if He wasn't calling me and I entered this field, I would do more harm than good.

When I was 16 years old, I went to the Police Station and talked with the Chief of Police W.I. Burden. I was curious about whether any school courses would help me in this field. Chief Burden advised me to finish school, and the Police Department had its own school.

Time went by. In the 11th grade I took Distributive Education and part of this course was having a job, so I went to work with Western Union Telegraph Co. I worked as a messenger boy until after graduation from High School. I was promoted to Operator and transferred to Aiken, where I stayed for about a year. Then I left them and started working as Night Auditor at the Calhoun Hotel, where I stayed for almost five years.

On April 6, 1963, I was married. My mother-in-law was keeping foster children and at that time, I believe she and her husband had about seven. In 1965, the courts placed a boy named Randy in foster care and because of his physical condition, it was hard to find someone to take care of him. Randy was a diabetic and only 11 years old. After learning of this, my wife and I decided to take him. We knew it would not be easy, as he needed a special diet and extra care. We managed, and Randy stayed with us for two years. He was placed with his sister for a while and then into two other foster homes. To cut it short, Randy is back with us now. We have four foster children at present, but for a good while, we had seven.

This column was somewhat personal, but I am glad to share my experiences with you. Pray for me that I will raise my own child right and for God to give me the wisdom and knowledge I need.

What Is a Cop?

(Dated Feb. 20, 1969)

If I were a salesman, I would try to build up that profession, but I am a cop.

No, this isn't a Dragnet script, but it is about cops. I know most cops would rather be called policemen. Personally, either one is all right with me.

If someone should ask, "What is a cop?" I would turn to a veteran police officer for the answer. Here, in his own words, is the answer of Dept. Inspector Conrad S. Jensen, retired member of the New York City Police Department.

"Cops are human (believe it or not), just like the rest of us. They come in both sexes, but mostly male. They also come in various sizes. This sometimes depends on whether you are looking for one or trying to hide something. However, they are mostly big.

"Cops are found everywhere—on land, on the sea, in the air, on horses, in cars, sometimes in your hair. In spite of the fact that 'you can't find one when you want one,' they are usually there when it counts most. The best way to get one is to pick up the phone.

"Cops deliver lectures, babies, and bad news. They are required to have the wisdom of Solomon, the disposition of a lamb and muscles of steel and are often accused of having a heart to match. He's the one who rings the doorbell, swallows hard and announces the passing of a loved one, then spends the rest of the day wondering why he ever took such a 'crummy' job.

"On T.V., a cop is an oaf who couldn't find a bull fiddle in a phone booth. In real life he's expected to find a little blond boy 'about so high' in a crowd of a half million people. In fiction, he gets help from private eyes, reporters and 'who-dun-it' fans. In real life, mostly all he gets from the public is 'I didn't see nuttin.'

"When he serves a summons, he's a monster. If he lets you go, he's a doll. To little kids, he's either a friend or a bogeyman, depending on how the parents feel about it. He works 'around the clock,' split shifts, etc. When he makes a mistake, 'he's a grafter and that goes for the rest of them, too.' When he shoots a stick-up man, he's a hero, except when the stick-up man is 'only a kid, anybody coulda seen that.'

"Lots of them have homes, some of them covered with ivy, but most of them covered with mortgages. If he drives a big car, he's a chisler; a little car, 'who's he kidding?' His credit is good, this is very helpful because his salary isn't. Cops raise lots of kids; most of them belong to other people.

"A cop sees more misery, bloodshed, trouble, and sunrises than the average person. Like the postman, cops must also be out in all kinds of weather. His uniform changes with the climate, but his outlook on life remains about the same; mostly a blank, but hoping for a better world.

"Cops like days off, vacations and coffee. They don't like auto horns, family fights, and anonymous letter writers. They have unions, but they can't strike. They must be impartial, courteous, and always remember the slogan 'at your service.' This is sometimes hard, especially when a character reminds him 'I'm a taxpayer. I pay your salary.'

"Cops get medals for saving lives, stopping runaway horses and shooting it out with bandits (once in a while his widow gets the medal). But sometimes the most rewarding moment comes when, after some small kindness to an older person, he feels the warm hand clasp, looks into grateful eyes and hears, 'Thank you and God bless you, son.'"

✴✴✴✴✴✴✴✴✴

I would like to thank Patrolman Tom King who provided me with this fine literature. Tom has been with the city for 30 odd years. He is a fine officer and a good Christian. I rode with Tom one night and was amazed at his deep knowledge of the Bible. I shall never forget that, and I will always have the highest respect for Tom. It's a pleasure to be working in the same department with him.

Race Relations

(Dated Feb. 27, 1969)

How many conversations have you heard start with the words "you know"? Well, this week I will try to write about something that perhaps you don't know about.

A visit to the Federal Penitentiary in Atlanta, Ga. is certainly enlightening. Looking into the faces of men and women, seeing a father visiting his son or a wife visiting her husband, and the most heart-breaking of all, seeing youngsters look at their father. I wonder where they went wrong. Some of the men had sentences as high as 340 years.

The prison is well-built and clean, but of course, the inmates would rather be home.

The second thing I have been thinking about lately is Church Street here in Anderson. The hostile feeling against the policemen on this street makes a tough job even harder. When they try to gang up on a policeman who is breaking up a fight, and just doing his job, well the least you can say is you certainly feel unwanted. This is a job for a good Negro policeman, but there is no one who wants it. So the resentment against a white policeman continues. It's commonplace to see a Negro lying in the street bleeding to death with a crowd of his own race just standing around not offering any kind of help.

It's hard for a policeman to see anyone in pain, and it comes naturally to want to help.

In Anderson we have about 25 percent Negro population, but at least 80 percent of the police calls come from the Negro sections.

There are some blacks who want to help their people and consider the policeman as a friend, instead of an enemy. Unfortunately there are so few of them, they are vastly outnumbered.

I would like to encourage the young colored men to put in applications for police work. There would be no prejudice against them from their co-workers, and they would better serve their own race who wouldn't be nearly as resentful of them.

What are your ideas along these lines? I would like to hear them. Even if you tell me to drop dead, as least I will know how the public feels about the situation. See you next week.

Bad Movies and Teens

(No date)

I have written articles concerning filthy movies being shown here. I don't know if my writing has drawn much attention to this situation or not, but at least some people are asking what can be done, and that certainly is the first step.

Some churches have blamed this on the new administration, and I would like to clear that up. All of the drive-ins are outside of the city, and the city administration has nothing to do with them. They don't have any authority in the county. With just 10 interested people, I could find out what we can do to stop the showing of such trash.

The juvenile authority has a repeater. A 14-year-old boy went before the juvenile authority last week. He was put on probation and then during the weekend, he was arrested for being drunk in public. Maybe two more years of probation added to what he already has will do some good. If it doesn't, he can always be put on four years' probation. I personally don't feel that this probation does a great amount of good. I know a boy who was sent to a school for boys for nine months, and it straightened him out.

Here in Anderson, the teenage problem is getting worse. I have said that it's not always the teenagers at fault, but the examples set by their parents. The other night, Officer Charles Partain and I received a call that there was a drunk man out in the street. When we arrived, nobody was in the street. A man was sitting on the porch and was drinking, but was not intoxicated. His wife staggered out of the house and demanded we lock up her husband. We could see that she was drunker than he was.

"If you don't lock him up, you need not come back," she said. "Just send the furniture company out." She meant

funeral home, but didn't know what she was saying. There is a 12-year-old daughter being reared in this home, and how will she turn out in such an atmosphere and environment?

Parents have got to stick together and make a strong attempt to bring up their children in the right way. There was a case last week of a boy who had been expelled from school. He went home and told his mother, who said the father would be furious at this news. She told the boy to leave the next day as if he were going to school and not let the father know he had been expelled. Instead of hiding the fact, she and the father should have worked together to get the boy back into school.

Back to the first subject of the column, filthy movies. I have talked with Senator Ed Garrison, and he seemed concerned about the situation. He advised me to go to a magistrate and take out a warrant, which I intend to do. I hope I can get enough people behind me to do some good. Getting these movies off the screen, putting a stop to teenagers getting beer and dope and giving them a decent type of recreation would help bring a big change for the better.

Teenagers are drinking and fighting with knives and guns. Eleven were jailed at one clip the other night, most of them under 20 and part of them under 18.

Church Involvement Needed

(No date)

You know, every time a law enforcement officer makes a mistake, it takes no time for word of this to spread. On the other hand, when a law enforcement officer does something good, there is only a small mention of it.

I would like to extend a pat on the back to Ben Harris for his quick thinking that changed what could have been a bad situation into a minor incident.

A large crowd had gathered in a downtown café, with both whites and blacks there. A fight over a small thing nearly developed between the members of the two races. Ben stopped this incident in a professional manner.

I guess I am bragging about the Police Department. So let me acknowledge others who do a good job: Members of the Anderson Fire Department and the Volunteer Fire Stations and Rescue Squads throughout the county. They all do a great work, some of them on a strictly volunteer basis.

A few words in closing (I said that once and then wrote three pages): Some of the movies being shown at our drive-in theaters are films that once would have been shown only at private parties, and the only way to describe them is "trash." I am surprised that these pictures are allowed in the county. A person visiting here and seeing the movies that are shown would think residents are low in morals.

Once I liked to go to the movies, but they are just too filthy now. How can we expect our kids to act any better when they see sex movies, beer drinking, and other vices flaunted in front of their eyes. I would like to see some church groups take an active interest in a protest against such movies as the ones being shown and marked "Adult Entertainment."

Help the Kids

(Dated March 20, 1969)

I write and wonder. Wonder if I am accomplishing anything by writing. Maybe if I were a school teacher or in some other profession, I would see the side of a teenager that

I know exists—the good side. Being a policeman, it's always the bad side of every situation that I see.

Then here goes another story of the bad side. It starts the same way all the other stories begin.

About 1 A.M., Officer Charles Partain and I were patrolling in the downtown section of town when we observed a car going north on Main Street at a high rate of speed, definitely a traffic case if we wanted to make one.

The driver of the car was 16 years old and pleaded for a break. We probably would have let him off with just a lecture, but we spotted several empty beer cans and two cans nearly full. There were four boys in the car, and two of them were old enough (legally) to drink. The others were not.

Again the 16-year-old driver pleaded for leniency as he only has four points left on his driver's license.

The father explained that he wasn't aware that the boy was having a problem until he ran across a letter from the Highway Department telling about the points. He stated that as far as he was concerned, the boy had proved he had no business driving a car.

He was appreciative of our help, and so were the parents of the other three boys. They all promised the boys would be dealt with accordingly.

The parents seemed sincere, and they convinced us they would do their best in the situation.

It seems that these teenagers do have a legitimate complaint when they say there is nothing worthwhile to do in Anderson. But the way some of them get their kicks is against the law. One night several fires were started, and teenagers were seen in the vicinity. Nearly 60 acres burned in one location. One teenager was stopped for running a fire truck off the road. As his excuse, he told us he knew it was against the law to follow a fire truck, so he was going around it.

In regard to last week's column regarding the filthy movies being shown at the drive-in theaters, we received some response. I believe that the churches are beginning to wake up, and I pray that something will be done.

I have to repeat that we cannot expect more from our kids when we allow a man to sell beer to teenagers without protesting, and allow trash to be shown on the movie screens. Merely saying it is a shame is a start, but let's do more. Set a good example for your kids, and let them know what you believe in.

Reputation and Character

(Dated March 27, 1969)

This article is not written with the intention of defending a man, or of convicting him. I am not a judge. Perhaps I can write it in such a manner that people will say, "If he is guilty, he should do this, or if he is innocent, he should do this."

According to the law, and that is what we must go by, every man is innocent until proven guilty. So let's assume the man is innocent.

Feelings are pretty strong now, concerning this man.

It could be any man. Don't say it couldn't be you because "I wouldn't do anything like that." Remember, every man is innocent until proven guilty, and an innocent man can be falsely accused. Simply being accused should not ruin a man's reputation, but it often does. Reputation is what people think of you; character is what you are. So it is possible to ruin the reputation while the character remains the same.

At this point, completely disregard the man and think only of what he is accused of doing. If a man is accused of running around with another man's wife, can there be circumstances to justify the situation? Personally, I say no. The Bible calls it adultery and speaks plainly, "Thou shall not commit adultery." And in Matthew the fifth chapter, we read: "But I say unto you, that whosoever looketh on a woman to lust after her hath committed adultery with her already in his heart. It has been said, whosoever shall put away his wife, let him give her a writing of divorcement, but I say unto you, that whosoever shall put away his wife, saving for the cause of fornication, causeth her to commit adultery; and whosoever shall marry her that is divorced, committeth adultery."

Thus, according to the Bible, it's wrong to go with another man's wife. Plain common sense would tell you this, even if you did not read the Bible.

Okay, so far we know that if the man has done what he is accused of doing, then he is wrong. His position cannot change that. It can't be wrong for one man and right for another.

If he isn't guilty, he should deny all charges vigorously. Public officials should set an example for other citizens. How can our children respect public officials when some of the examples they set are unacceptable to any except low characters?

Again, let me repeat that this man has been accused only. He hasn't been convicted; he has not confessed. One thought to bear in mind: "Judge not that ye be not judged."

Wake Up, Parents!

(Dated April 10, 1969)

This article is more frank than others I have written concerning teenagers. Some of you may not believe these facts.

Everyone keeps saying, "Teenagers are no different now than 10 years ago." They say, "Boys will be boys." "Let them have their fun. Let them sow their wild oats." That's what the fathers of the boys say. Or the father of a lovely daughter knows there are bad girls, but they belong to the man down the street. "My girl wouldn't do anything like that."

Wake up, parents. Within the last two months, nine couples have been caught in raids, in a shameful act, and completely in the nude. Readers, this was right here in Anderson, not somewhere else. These are YOUR teenagers, not someone else's.

A few years ago, there was talk of a sex club. You remember the rules. To be a member, a girl had to seduce two married men and have illicit relationships with them.

Perhaps you don't believe that happened, or that it could be happening again.

I think that these filthy sex movies definitely have an effect on the teenagers. Selling beer to minors contributes to the downfall of the juveniles, too.

"What is wrong with a youngster drinking beer?" a father questioned me. "I have beer around the house, and I hope he can hold his beer as well as I can when it comes time for him to drink."

If you think I'm making this up, you are wrong. Some parents want their children to drink, or they laugh and don't care when they find out they do drink.

Police Officer Charles Partain and I were called out to a country road where a group of teenagers had pulled up close to a house and started cursing, fighting, and generally creating a disturbance. When we got there, they were still going at it. You could smell the beer, but you couldn't tell which boys were drinking it. We carried them to the police station and called their parents.

One of the parents told us to hold up about the drinking unless we could prove which boys had been drinking. We charged the boys with disorderly conduct, and the next morning, the boys and all of the parents were present for a hearing.

The parents seemed like decent folks, and they wanted to do the right thing. The man who had called the police said he didn't wish them prosecuted and ne ther did Officer Partain nor myself. The judge gave them a good talking to, and the parents assured us the boys would be dealt with accordingly.

It is just so important to give kids more wholesome recreation, and to figure out a way to keep them away from beer. Anyone selling beer to minors should have action brought against them.

We have got to take the temptations away and replace them with more worthwhile activities. They can have fun in better ways, but churches and individuals have got to open the door, help them, and show them that we care.

One night Paul and his partner got a call to go to the Emergency Room to interview a man who had been stabbed. While he was there, a nurse told him how much she enjoyed his columns. She stated she agreed with him 100% about teenagers drinking. Then she added, "We keep beer in the refrigerator, but our kids know better than to touch it." Paul's immediate thought was, "I know what next week's column will be. How can parents tell their kids drinking is wrong when they do it themselves? They have to set the example."

Who Is to Blame?

(Dated May 1, 1969)

"Train up a child in the way he should go, and when he is old, he will not depart from it."

Keep that theme in mind throughout this article, and remember that adults were once kids.

I would like to ask a question or two, and you can answer for yourself. "What type of parent will the teenagers we have now make in the near future?" The near future is nearer than you think.

Another question: "Who is to blame?" I know you think, as I do, that there are some kids who are mean as snakes who have pretty good parents, and there are some pretty good kids with sorry parents. But as a general rule, when the parents are the right kind and they make a little extra effort to see their kids growing up properly, everything goes well. When a boy or girl gets into one thing right after the other, I don't believe the parents are taking the right corrective measures.

How can a man sitting in a beer joint, drinking beer, say his kids go to church and believe everything is all right? This man knows what is right for that boy or girl. He tries to get his kids to church, but he never goes himself.

He is not living what he is preaching. I needed the church when I was young, and I need it even more now. The person who just sends his children to church is saying, "Son, or Daughter, you go to church now, but when you get as old as your mother and I are, you won't have to go. You won't need the Lord then."

How wrong they are. The parents who get drunk on the weekend and attempt to send their boy or girl to church, shouldn't be surprised when that boy or girl no longer goes to church but starts drinking instead.

Here in Anderson, the teenagers need some decent form of recreation, but what they need more than anything else is a good example. I understand a very strong effort is being made by Mayor Rich Otter to give the teenagers some form of recreation. A drag strip is in the thinking stage. I believe, if properly supervised, it would be good thing. Kids have more energy now than ever before, and they need something elaborate on which they can expend that energy.

On a call to investigate family trouble, we found a man who couldn't do anything to straighten out his kids. The parents have not lived the right sort of life before their children, and listening to the situation, it seemed they [the children] were doing all right, considering the mess they were brought up in. The daughter was dating an older man, supposedly divorced, and the father didn't like for his daughter to date this person. He wanted to see papers to prove there had been a divorce. Frankly, I wouldn't want a 17-year-old daughter dating this man, even if he were divorced. I advised the parents to go to church, read the Bible with the children, and pray with them.

On another call, the father was in a drunken rage about the late hours the daughter was keeping. The mother argued, "No wonder they stay out late. Only a maniac would attempt to molest his own daughter." She told the police he had bothered every female in the house and had even tried to molest the family dog.

Another case deals with a father being drunk, and his three-year-old son had a strong smell of alcohol on his breath.

These things happen right here in Anderson. I see it. The coroner could tell you some stories that would curl the hair on a bald head.

I am proud that some of the churches are taking measures to stop the filthy movies on our screens. A petition is going around. I hope you will sign it when it comes to your church.

Let us set the proper example before these kids. They need help. Some of these adults I have mentioned are probably beyond help, but it's not too late for the teenagers.

Movies and Troubled Youth

(No date)

Last week, I talked about the need to stop the filthy movies being shown, and was very pleased with the response. Now I know there are many people who would like to see these movies disappear from our local screens. Some of them feel that efforts so far have been a waste of time, but let me assure you that I haven't finished.

I called Senator Ed Garrison, and he advised me to go to a magistrate and take out a warrant for the operators of the drive-in theaters. When I talked to the magistrate, he admitted that something needed to be done, but said he didn't know what statutes would cover the situation. So I called Senator Garrison again, and he said he would contact the Attorney General for a new ruling on this. A letter, which I shall publish in The Free Press within the next two weeks or as soon as I hear from him, will follow.

I asked for 10 active supporters and so far I have six, including a father of the Catholic Church, a lawyer's wife, and a policeman.

Item No. 2 for today deals with Mother's Day and of one mother I know who was sad on that day for her son was in jail. She was forced to sign a warrant against him, after begging him to straighten out. The son is in his 50s and the mother is 75 years old. She was crying her eyes out as she signed the warrant. In court, the mother told the judge what had happened and stated that she loved her son.

As she started out of the courtroom, she threw her arms around her son and expressed her sorrow and love. The son had been quite hostile to his mother while under the influence of alcohol. After becoming sober, he admitted he had to quit drinking. He will spend 10 days with the county.

Item No. 3 deals with events of Friday night. About 12:30, my wife called the Police Station stating there had been an auto accident right in front of our home. Officer Partain and I were sent to stand by until Patrolman Hershel Childs arrived to investigate the incident. Officer Childs is a traffic officer. There were three boys in the car, one was about 17 and the others 12 and 15. There was a strong odor of alcohol.

Later on in the night, we received a couple of prowler calls. When we arrived, we found a 15-year-old boy on a man's porch. He acted strange as if he had been sniffing glue and couldn't remember where he lived. He didn't have any idea of the time or where he was. We carried him to the police station where the phone was ringing again. It was the same house and a lady was screaming on the phone. Another boy was there, insisting he lived there and that he had seen his mother go into the house. We called his home and his mother and father came to the station. Both boys were about 15. The last boy insisted his mother was lying and that he HAD seen her going into the house. It was obvious both were in a highly emotional state, brought on by either glue-sniffing or some drug.

Section 16-417-7

(No date)

Last week I stated that I would publish a letter from the Attorney General's office regarding filthy movies. The letter, dated May 13, reads as follows:

"Dear Mr. Jordan: Senator Ed Garrison has asked that I refer you to the statutes in this state which relate to prosecutions for the distribution of obscene matter and I am enclosing herewith a copy of the statute relating to such matters.

"The statute covers motion pictures, except those which carry the Motion Picture Association of America's code seal of approval and covers any other means by which obscene matter may be possessed or exhibited.

"I direct your attention particularly to the fact that a prosecution for violation of the statute will most probably be successful where obscene matter is made available to minors under the age of sixteen. The particular statute involved is Section 16-414-3 which is a part of the document enclosed herewith.

"There are also provisions for obtaining search warrants for obscene matter, the procedure for which is set forth in Section 16-414-7.

"With all best wishes, Very Truly Yours, Daniel R. McLeod, Attorney General."

Section 16-414-3 of this statute reads: "It shall be unlawful for any person who, with knowledge that a person is a minor under sixteen years of age, or who, while in possession of such facts that he should reasonably know that such person is a minor under the age of sixteen years of age, knowingly to send or cause to be sent, exhibit, distribute or offer to distribute any obscene matter to such minors."

In Section 16-414-4 of the same statute regarding the employment of minors to work at such places: "It shall be unlawful for any person, who with knowledge that a person is a minor under sixteen years of age, or who, while in possession of such facts that he should reasonably know that such person is a minor under sixteen years of age, to hire, employ or to use such minor to do or assist in doing any of the acts prohibited by section 16-414-1 to 16-414-9."

Before getting any deeper into this matter, let me ask this. Have you ever seen a kid taking up tickets under sixteen years of age at these movies? I have seen kids working there while the decent movies were playing. I don't know whether they work on the "dirty movie" nights or not.

Section 16-414-5 deals with advertising: "It shall be unlawful for any person to write or to create obscene advertising or to solicit anyone to publish such advertising or otherwise to promote the sale or distribution of such matter."

In reference to news stands or places where magazines or other obscene literature is sold, Section 16-414-6 reads: "It shall be unlawful for any person knowingly to require as a condition to a sale, allocation, consignment or delivery for resale of any paper, magazine, book, periodical, publication or other merchandise that the purchaser or consignee receive any obscene matter or to deny or threaten to revoke, or to impose any penalty, financial or otherwise.

High-Speed Chase

(Dated May 29, 1969)

The response on the drive-in theater question has been gratifying, and we hope to have another answer in the next issue.

On the beat at 12 o'clock on a Saturday night, Patrolman Cal McCullough and I were checking out a service station at the corner of Whitner and Tower, when a car turned off Whitner onto Tower cutting across the service station lot in front of us in a burst of speed. Attempting to stop the car for speeding, we got pretty close at Tower and Market, when the driver sped up leaving us behind.

We could tell there were teenagers in the car and that they were white. It was a 1962 Buick, and until the driver attempted to escape, all we could have booked him for was a minor traffic violation (as far as we knew).

He was driving at such a high rate of speed we could not get close enough to get his license number. When he crossed the street, the car was fish-tailing, we found out later from the passenger in the car, who said he tried unsuccessfully to get the driver to stop. He barely missed a collision with another car, Officer McCullough said, while I kept watching the road while driving. When we hit the city limits, I decided to let him go, rather than risk any lives in a continuance of the high-speed pursuit. Suddenly ahead we saw the whole sky light up with fire that seemed to be everywhere, and we knew they had wrecked.

We called the county officers to direct them to the scene where wires were all over the road and a telephone pole was cut in half. This was a pole with a transformer on it, so we

113

stopped a pretty long way from the wreck to avoid the hot lines. The car was in a yard, and a teenager was out walking around in a daze, looking for something. We asked him where the other boy was, and he said he had looked in the car, under the car, and all around and couldn't find him. By that time a crowd was gathering, and we started a search of the area for the other boy. He was spotted lying near some bushes, and someone hollered, "He needs an ambulance. He's hurt pretty bad." We didn't attempt to move him, but in a few minutes he opened his eyes, and there was a shocked look on his face. We told him to lie still, and some of his panic seemed to subside. After getting his name and assisting the county deputies, we went over to look at the car.

The car was in one yard, and the door from the car in a neighbor's yard. When the ambulance arrived, we were at one end of the street, directing traffic to turn around where the hot wires were on the ground.

The passenger told us the other boy had picked him up around 9 P.M. and that since that time, he had consumed at least nine beers and some whiskey.

There were three different stories here. The police, the teenagers, and the boy's father all played parts. If the father had not allowed the boy to drive in his condition none of this would have happened. If the boy had not driven in a reckless manner, the police would never have been involved.

If I had not agreed to work extra, I would never have been involved in a high-speed chase. Perhaps I could have overtaken the boy before the wreck, but I assumed that if I stopped the chase, he would slow down. I wanted to save the lives of the boy and his passenger, as well as those of Officer McCullough and myself.

The driver is a patient in the hospital, but he is lucky. He might have been a grim statistic in the automobile fatalities list.

Alcohol and Accidents

(No date)

According to the Scriptures, "Whatsoever a man soweth that shall he also reap."

Every day we see evidence of this. Ask several officers who saw a perfect example. A man running a beer joint has his son helping him and both got involved in a situation, fighting with knives and sticks. The son had to have several stitches taken to his face.

They were not fighting each other. The son became involved in a dispute with another man at the father's place of business.

In the emergency room, the father and mother of the young man seemed proud as their son kept asking, "How many of them did it take to hold me off?"

He had been raised to hold his liquor as good as his parents. How much better off would he have been had his parents owned a grocery store or another type of business?

I had rather starve to death than to make a living selling whiskey or beer. But somebody will sell it. A fight might have occurred at a grocery store, but the odds are certainly more in favor of it happening at a beer joint.

Wasted lives are sad. The recent death of a woman who spent her life around beer halls made me think of her children. The daughter has a terrible reputation, the son died drunk.

I have never seen a heavy drinker who will not admit that he ought to quit drinking.

Last week I wrote about a drunken driver who asked for a jury trial and got off. Some other officers told me not to feel bad about it. The same man has been charged before, asked for jury trials and been turned loose. He has a great deal of money, so I guess he can do as he pleases. He will probably have to pay somebody a high settlement some day when he runs over a child.

However, I will continue doing my job to the best of my ability. A policeman doesn't get a bonus for making cases. Quite the contrary—it costs him time, his own time. He has to go to court to try to convict the person.

Many citizens don't know that a blood test for alcohol content is not given unless a defendant asks for it and pays for it himself. And then this test cannot be used against him in court. A man who is too drunk to make a telephone call is turned loose by a jury because he didn't get to make his allotted phone call.

Not many people involved in traffic accidents are ever charged with driving under the influence, whether this is the case of not.

Too often, the impact of hitting another car and going into shock makes a driver appear intoxicated. It is difficult, therefore, to make charges like this stick.

Two "false alarm bugs" were apprehended the other night. When asked why they did it, one of them replied, "Well, we didn't have anything else to do."

Parent-Children Conflict

(No date)

A while back I wrote about a man and woman with two kids they did not want. I already have signed a petition against these parents, and it is currently under investigation by the Juvenile Court.

The other night Patrolman Charles Partain of the Police Department, Randy Martin of the Juvenile Office, and I were again given a first-hand example of these two adults' conduct. They still maintain they will sign anything to get the two kids out of their hair, so to speak.

I have observed several cases where kids ran away from home for some reason or another, but it was always the kid's idea to leave—not the parents'. This case is different, though. The parents don't want the kids. The kids said they loved their parents but that they were at the end of the road. I just hope the proper decision can be reached when this case comes before the court.

The new city administration is having somewhat of a problem with the Sanitation Department insofar as complaints received about garbage pick-up. I believe constructive suggestions would be appreciated, as I have found city officials to be very open-minded and easy to talk to.

This administration has actually ridden the garbage trucks in an effort to see what is wrong. The Sanitation Department has problems just as every city department and most business firms do.

I shall close with a passage I sincerely believe: "Seek ye first the kingdom of God and his righteousness and all these things shall be added unto you."

Acquittal Because of Publicity?

(No date)

I guess it would be proper for me to apologize to Patrolman Johnny Getsinger. It seems a previous article by me in The Free Press has become the basis for acquittal of a young man Patrolman Getsinger arrested for reckless driving.

The case originated several months ago. Getsinger was working extra duty at Belvedere Plaza. A young man was noted doing a lot of reckless driving in that section. Police cars had been alerted. Getsinger did not have a police radio, but he saw the car and could identify the driver. He also witnessed the reckless manner in which the car was being driven.

Later the car was stopped by Patrolman Getsinger and the driver was charged with reckless driving. He was given until the next day to arrange bond, but he made no effort. Finally, two weeks later, police had to go and pick him up. Then bond was posted and a request made for a jury trial.

As of this week, that jury trial has not been set. A lawyer obtained by the youth appeared before Judge Richard Ruhle and asked that the case be thrown out on grounds the defendant couldn't possibly get a fair trial in Anderson due to the article in The Anderson Free Press.

The lawyer didn't say his client was innocent. He merely stated that due to the publicity about the case his client couldn't possibly get a fair trial.

If this were a murder case, maybe one could better understand, but a case of reckless driving with bond set as low as $52! To the police officer, it is not a case of providing $52 to the city, but of principle. No person, whether of high or low income, has the right to break the law and get away with it.

The defendant could have paid the $52—like most do when charged with traffic violations—and avoided the cost of a lawyer and the trouble of going to court.

It leads me to one conclusion: since reckless driving takes off six points under state law—maybe the driver didn't have six points to spare.

Perhaps this article will give his lawyer more grounds for acquittal. But allow me at this point to say Judge Ruhle didn't figure the grounds were sufficient to acquit and has sent the case to a higher court. Even if the case is lost, policemen are assured that Judge Ruhle is behind doing what is right. That is the way it should be.

Policemen can make mistakes like any human, but no man regardless of color, regardless of how important he is, or anything else has the right to break the law and get away with it. Such does not hurt just one citizen, but all citizens. It weakens the law, and the way the Supreme Court has already weakened laws, it won't be long before there won't be any law and order at all.

Frustration

(No date)

Here goes another complaint.

It is almost impossible to convict a drunk driver. When a person asks for a jury trial, he's really putting the arresting officer on trial.

The policeman is asked what happened and he starts off, "We received a call..." when the defense lawyer objects. The objection: "Don't tell what anybody else received, just what you did."

The policeman starts again, "As the result of a call given to all city and county units...." Objection: "You can't tell it that way. You don't know what the other cars received."

Let me get that lawyer out by the next paragraph and maybe I can say a word or two without being interrupted.

Ben Turner, the radio dispatcher for the city, put out a call, addressing it to both the city and county units to be on the look-out for a blue Chevrolet pickup truck, heading north on Main Street.

I never could say this in court, and probably some of the people sitting on the jury wondered why I stopped the truck in the first place.

The report was that the truck driver was drunk. I was near the Calhoun Hotel on North Main when I spotted the truck. Getting the call didn't give me an excuse to stop the man without first observing him. Knowing that I might have to testify how the man was driving, I followed the truck a few blocks, noticing that it stayed on the wrong side of the road. I turned my blue light on, and the siren, and attempted to pull the truck over. This went on for three blocks without him stopping, then he had to stop for a stop sign. Thank goodness he didn't run it. I jumped out, and asked the man to show me his driver's license. He got out stumbling against the truck and using it for a prop. His speech was slurred, and there was a strong odor of alcohol. He had difficulty in standing. So I arrested him for driving under the influence.

Another officer testified as to his condition only minutes after he had gotten out of the truck. His testimony was that the man was highly intoxicated.

Neither policeman's word was good enough for the jury. A man was put on the stand and testified that he saw the man just a few minutes after he was arrested and he was completely sober. The defendant's testimony was that his eyes had been burned and he couldn't see clearly, which would account for his driving on the wrong side of the road.

The jury wanted to know if the man had been given a blood test. The question wasn't allowed.

What do you think? Do you think there was sufficient evidence to convict or is there a reasonable doubt in your mind?

The jury found this man not guilty. To my way of thinking, a jury trial is often just a joke. It would be ironic if the man were out driving one day in this condition and a member of the jury who freed him happened to get in his way.

Drugs and Glue Sniffing

(Dated Jan. 15, 1970)

With all of the ice and cold weather, things have been somewhat quiet during the past week. Working a little extra time at Belvedere Plaza Saturday night would have been extremely quiet except for three boys.

They were drinking beer and driving through a hamburger place. I had to place two of the boys under arrest, and carried them inside the building to call the Police Department. Under a city ordinance prohibiting drinking in public, I asked for a car to carry the two boys to jail.

They gave me two names, then I looked outside to see if the car was coming. When I turned around, the boys were gone. They ran out the back door, and I saw them running across a car lot nearby. In checking around, I found that the names given me by the boys were false, but I soon found out who they were, anyway. One of them had already been involved in several violations of the law.

On Sunday night, Officer Partain went along with me to Central Presbyterian Church where we had the privilege of talking to the young people. It was a pleasure to see these youngsters at church. A few of them agreed to be on our radio program Saturday morning, and we taped the program that Sunday night at the church.

Patrolman Partain had secured information on different types of drugs and glue sniffing. He also had access to movies showing the harmful effects of these items. He stated that he would be happy to show these movies and his drug display to any group. Anyone interested can contact me or Officer Partain and we will attempt to fill all requests for enlightenment on the dangers of drugs.

An article entitled "City Police Open Drive Against Glue Sniffing" was published after this in The Anderson Free Press. It included the following information:

The possibility of a future city ordinance helping to regulate the glue sniffing situation was mentioned by Mayor Richard Otter, who announced that about two dozen letters are to be mailed to drug stores, department stores, sports and hobby shops, five and dime stores, and other merchants falling into the category of handling glue sales.

Since no state statutes or city ordinances on glue sniffing are known by the city administration to exist in the state, such an ordinance if passed in Anderson would constitute "ground breaking" into the area of control of glue sniffing....

"The children we have seen involved in this have appeared to have serious mental and physical difficulties," Mayor Otter said.... "These youngsters were in pitiful shape mentally and physically. Some were disturbed and very emaciated in appearance."

Free Speech?

This article that appeared in a local publication and then was quoted here by The Anderson Free Press describes the attack on Paul's right of free speech.

An interesting editorial concerning an Anderson policeman recently appeared in The Anderson Free Press. The article reads as follows:

POLICEMAN CAN WRITE

"A misunderstanding in the Welfare Department almost brought an end to the writing endeavors of an Anderson policeman whose comments published in The Free Press in recent weeks have drawn wide attention.

"Patrolman Paul Jordan, a foster parent approved by the Welfare Department, was advised by an employee of the Welfare Department that he 'couldn't get involved in politics' and be a foster parent, too.

"Jordan and his wife are the foster parents of seven children. He said he was advised that a foster parent is considered an employee of the Welfare Department and, therefore, was not permitted to become involved in politics. The policeman said he was told that his writings appearing in The Free Press had been sent to the State Welfare Department in Columbia, which ruled against him publicly expressing himself.

"In the articles, Jordan said after being told he could no longer write them... 'I have seven kids at my house—seven foster children I have learned to love. I don't want to ever lose them, for I feel like they are my own, and I wouldn't take anything for them.'

"Rather than face losing his foster children, Jordan agreed to give up writing. But as it turned out, he didn't have to give up either.

"Jordan was later advised by the head of the local Welfare Department that he could continue to express himself in articles published in the newspaper."

Free speech, guaranteed in the Constitution, was attacked, but Free Speech prevailed.

Political Campaign

In 1972, the Republican Party persuaded Paul to run for Coroner of Anderson County. Though the registered Democrats greatly outnumbered the Republicans, he decided to give it a try. The Republican Party financed his campaign for the office, so he took a three-week leave from his police duties to campaign. He recruited Clyde and a young boy named Randy to help him put out posters and deliver flyers to hundreds of houses. They did this in the city of Anderson and in the surrounding small towns in the county.

The pastor of a church in Starr invited him to come speak to his congregation on a Sunday night, and Paul promised to be there. Before Sunday night came, he was notified that Channel 4 TV would interview the candidates that same night, thereby giving them more exposure over the entire county than they could get in any other way. It would be a golden opportunity for Paul to make his case for his qualifications. What a predicament he was in—how could he pass up this golden opportunity, yet he had given his word to the pastor in Starr? The RIGHT thing to do would be to keep his word and speak at the church in Starr. So he did.

The photo of him below, showing him with a gun in one hand and the Bible in the other, is one that was used in the campaign. He wanted to show that he would never be bribed to make a false decision, but would always be guided by God.

Unfortunately, he did not win the election. However, while he was at the poll, an insurance agent he knew saw him and asked him to consider working for her company, Independent Life. After giving it some thought, he decided to talk with her manager about it. Afterwards, he showed the Chief that he could make twice the salary he was making with the Police Department, and the Chief said he couldn't blame him for making the change. The Chief expressed his regrets that he couldn't pay him enough to keep him, but gave his blessing for the move.

Paul worked out his notice and was then sent to school in Atlanta to be trained for work at the Independent Life Insurance Company. His new career had begun.

Chapter Seven
New Career

In 1972, after eight and a half years as a policeman, Paul's salary was $6,700 per year. The job at Independent Life Insurance Company offered a salary exactly double that amount. Paul had been moonlighting as a Security Guard for extra money, sometimes working two extra jobs. Now he would only have to work one job, period.

It was while he was going through the one-week training classes in Atlanta that he realized what a big move he had made. He was no longer a policeman. Had he made the right move? Right or wrong, the decision had been made. Now he needed to look forward and not back. It was December of 1972, the end of one career and the beginning of another.

Independent Life Insurance

At Independent Life, he had a Debit, a route that was established with customers who had already purchased insurance from the company. His job was to collect the premium payments each month. Most people paid during the first week of the month, so he might have 60 or 70 stops to make each day for the first week. The next three weeks weren't quite as busy.

Someone from the insurance office travelled with him for the first three weeks, introducing him to the customers and showing him how to keep the payment records accurately. After that, he was on his own.

One aspect of the job was selling new policies to his customers or finding new customers. For this, he had to learn all of the details about the policies his company offered. He soon mastered this and was making good progress with new policies being sold.

Hazards

In the Police Department, there were the obvious hazards of being shot at or being injured when someone resisted arrest. Now conditions were different, but there were hazards just the same.

One hazard of the job was the many dogs that didn't know him, didn't want to know him, and who thought it was their express responsibility to scare him away from their yard—or chew him up, whichever. One customer lived on a hill, 75 to 80 feet up, with no driveway up the hill. This necessitated his parking at the bottom of the hill and avoiding getting eaten by the two Doberman dogs that accompanied him every step of the way up the long climb. He was advised to take dog biscuits with which to bribe them.

He threw each dog a biscuit at the bottom of the hill, and they eagerly went to work eating and ignoring him—for a few steps. "This is working. It's not so bad. I can do this," he thought. Then they were back for more, demanding and menacing. Uh oh, better throw out another biscuit. Success again. Over and over this worked, and he was feeling pretty confident—until he had no more biscuits, and there was still a lot of hill left. He thought pretending to throw something might work, and it did a couple of times, but these dogs were no dummies. They were fooled twice, but no more. Now they demanded the real thing.

All he could do was continue walking up the hill, the dogs snapping at his heels. One dog apparently thought he wasn't paying proper attention, and he was miffed because of Paul throwing his arm with no biscuit, so he grabbed Paul in the side.

At just that moment, the door opened and the owner called the dogs off. Whew! Saved his hide, actually, his side. The dog had just nipped and hadn't fastened down with his teeth, or it would have been a different story.

The owner had a good policy, and losing it would have cost Paul a considerable amount of his monthly income, so he figured he'd have to learn to cope. The obvious answer was more dog biscuits, lots more. He determined to never run out again.

Not long after, one of the dogs was run over by a car and killed, so his danger was cut in half. He knew the owner grieved over the loss of the dog, and he was sympathetic, but he was able to cut in half his expense for dog biscuits.

Other hazards included people who would tell him at 1 o'clock to please come back at 3, and at 3 when he went back, they would write him a check for the payment, something they could just as easily have done at 1.

Obviously there were times when the customer legitimately didn't have the money and needed to pay later, and he understood this, but....

Sometimes the hazard came in the form of a small boy, standing out in the yard, pointing to the window and saying, "Mama said to tell you she's not here."

The Police Department had furnished his uniforms and a patrol car while he was on duty. Now he furnished his own clothes, his own car, paid for his own gas, and there was no Carlos giving him half-priced meals. It wasn't as lucrative as it had sounded at first. Still, he made the best of it and just determined to sell more policies to increase his income.

Winning Trips

Each year the company would offer an all-expense-paid trip to a different large city for the agents who qualified. The requirements were to have an increase in volume, payment increases, a good low percentage in arrears, be consistently on schedule, etc. Usually out of 30 agents, five or six would qualify.

Paul qualified a number of years and won trips to San Antonio, San Francisco, Washington, DC, Atlanta, Boston, Lake Tahoe, Nevada, and New Orleans. On the New Orleans trip, Kim and Paula went along with him and Frances, so they drove. These trips really were ALL-expenses paid, so they made wonderful vacations.

Promotion

At one point, he was promoted to Staff Manager in the Whiteville, NC office. He put the house in Anderson up for sale and moved his family to NC. The title of Staff Manager carried with it a certain amount of prestige, but he soon learned that was about the only benefit. There were supposed to be six agents under him working that area, but when he arrived, there were two vacancies. Until he could hire replacements, he had to cover those two Debits (routes) himself, which was very time-consuming. Each one involved a lot of traveling, plus he was doing the work of three people: the two missing agents and the Staff Manager. As Staff Manager, he was supposed to travel some with each of the other agents, who also had widespread territories.

He toughed it out and stayed there for nine months, hiring about eighteen agents during that time, as one after the other, each Debit would come open. Agents simply couldn't afford to cover such widespread areas, as travel expenses were high, so there was rapid turnover.

When someone complained to his boss because he had started a Staff Meeting with prayer, asking God to bless their endeavors, the boss informed him that prayer was not allowed.

For the first six months, he was paying for housing in NC and back in SC, because it took that long to sell the house in Anderson. This had been a really special house, built by an architect for himself with lots of special features. Now when it was purchased, it was converted to a Nursing Home.

He decided he would give up the position of Staff Manager and go back to simply being an Agent, but when he asked to be moved back to Anderson, he was told by a secretary that there were no openings. After he had taken a position in Greenville and rented a house in nearby Simpsonville, he happened to talk with the Manager in Anderson who told him that had he known Paul was available to come back to Anderson, he would have made a spot for him. Too late. He had promised the Manager in Greenville that he would stick with him and not move back to Anderson when an opening became available, and he had signed a lease on the rental house.

When that lease was up, he did move his family back to Anderson, and they even moved back into a house they had owned a few years earlier.

License

Each year in August or September, the insurance company requires its agents to be tested in order to be licensed for the upcoming year. A lecture is given, and then the agents are tested, a score of 85 or above being required. Paul has learned the business and the policies he sells so well over the years that he could pass the test without the lecture, but he attends it, anyway. It always feels good to have a high score on any test.

Change Needed

After so many years of selling insurance, Paul wanted a change. He applied and was hired by Anderson County as a guard at the Detention Center. He gave the required two weeks' notice to Independent Life and looked forward to new challenges.

Accident

Before his two weeks' notice was finished, Paul was on a ladder, cleaning the gutters on his house, when the ladder slipped out from under him. He called for help while he clung to the gutter. By the time Frances, Kim, and Paula came running out of the house, he had lost his grip and fallen to the ground. He found he couldn't get up. An ambulance took him to the hospital, where it was found that he had broken two vertebrae, T-11 and T-12. His chest was strapped to hold the vertebrae in place, and he was kept on bed rest for eight days. He was released to go home with instructions to remain in bed so the bones could heal. By the time he was allowed up, he had to learn to walk again. He ended up out of work for eight months, during which time Independent Life continued to pay his salary. Even though he had given his notice, he was still employed by them at the time of the accident. He never did become a guard at the county Detention Center.

He wanted a job based in Anderson, so he went to work for Liberty Life Insurance, where he worked for three or four years. He had worked for Independent Life for 24 years, but 25 years would have meant he would receive a pension from the company, so they hired him back for the one remaining year needed. His work for them had been exemplary, so they were glad to have him back for any period of time.

Office Christmas Party

One year he was asked to give a devotional talk as the entertainment for the office Christmas party. He first recited from memory the Christmas story from Luke 1:26-2:21. It is printed below to show you what a long and beautiful passage this is.

And in the sixth month the angel Gabriel was sent from God unto a city of Galilee, named Nazareth.

To a virgin espoused to a man whose name was Joseph, of the house of David; and the virgin's name was Mary.

And the angel came in unto her, and said, Hail, thou that art highly favoured, the Lord is with thee: blessed art thou among women.

And when she saw him, she was troubled at his saying, and cast in her mind what manner of salutation this should be.

And the angel said unto her, Fear not, Mary: for thou hast found favour with God.

And, behold, thou shalt conceive in thy womb, and bring forth a son, and shalt call his name JESUS.

He shall be great, and shall be called the Son of the Highest: and the Lord God shall give unto him the throne of his father David:

And he shall reign over the house of Jacob forever; and of his kingdom there shall be no end.

Then said Mary unto the angel, How shall this be, seeing I know not a man?

And the angel answered and said unto her, The Holy Ghost shall come upon thee, and the power of the Highest shall over shadow thee: therefore also that holy thing which shall be born of thee shall be called the Son of God.

And, behold, thy cousin Elisabeth, she hath also conceived a son in her old age: and this is the sixth month with her, who was called barren.

For with God nothing shall be impossible. And Mary said, Behold the handmaid of the Lord; be it unto me according to thy word. And the angel departed from her.

And Mary arose in those days, and went into the hill country with haste, into a city of Judah;

And entered into the house of Zacharias, and saluted Elisabeth.

And it came to pass, that, when Elisabeth heard the salutation of Mary, the babe leaped in her womb; and Elisabeth was filled with the Holy Ghost;

And she spake out with a loud voice, and said, Blessed art thou among women, and blessed is the fruit of thy womb.

And whence is this to me, that the mother of my Lord should come to me?

For, lo, as soon as the voice of thy salutation sounded in mine ears, the babe leaped in my womb for joy.

And blessed is she that believed: for there shall be a performance of those things which were told her from the Lord.

And Mary said, My soul doth magnify the Lord.

And my spirit hath rejoiced in God my Saviour.

For he hath regarded the low estate of his handmaiden: for, behold, from henceforth all generations shall call me blessed.

For he that is mighty hath done to me great things; and holy is his name.

And his mercy is on them that fear him from generation to generation.

He hath shewed strength with his arm; he hath scattered the proud in the imagination of their hearts.

He hath put down the mighty from their seats, and exalted them of low degree.

He hath filled the hungry with good things; and the rich he hath sent empty away.

He hath holpen his servant Israel, in remembrance of his mercy;

As he spake to our fathers, to Abraham, and to his seed forever.

And Mary abode with her about three months, and returned to her own house.

Now Elisabeth's full time came that she should be delivered; and she brought forth a son.

And her neighbours and her cousins heard how the Lord had shewed great mercy upon her; and they rejoiced with her.

And it came to pass, that on the eighth day they came to circumcise the child; and they called him Zacharias, after the name of his father.

And his mother answered and said, Not so; but he shall be called John.

And they said unto her, There is none of thy kindred that is called by this name.

And they made signs to his father, how he would have him called.

And he asked for a writing table, and wrote, saying, His name is John. And they marveled all.

And his mouth was opened immediately, and his tongue loosed, and he spake, and praised God.

And fear came on all that dwelt round about them: and all these sayings were noised abroad throughout all the hill country of Judaea.

And all they that heard them laid them up in their hearts, saying, What manner of child shall this be! And the hand of the Lord was with him.

And his father Zacharias was filled with the Holy Ghost, and prophesied, saying,

Blessed be the Lord God of Israel; for he hath visited and redeemed his people,

And hath raised up a horn of salvation for us in the house of his servant David;

As he spake by the mouth of his holy prophets, which have been since the world began:

That we should be saved from our enemies, and from the hand of all that hate us;

To perform the mercy promised to our fathers, and to remember his holy covenant;

The oath which he sware to our father Abraham,

That he would grant unto us, that we being delivered out of the hand of our enemies might serve him without fear,

In holiness and righteousness before him, all the days of our life.

And thou, child, shall be called the prophet of the Highest: for thou shalt go before the face of the Lord to prepare his ways;

To give knowledge of salvation unto his people by the remission of their sins,

Through the tender mercy of our God; whereby the dayspring from on high hath visited us,

To give light to them that sit in darkness and in the shadow of death, to guide our feet into the way of peace.

And the child grew, and waxed strong in spirit, and was in the deserts till the day of his shewing unto Israel.

Chapter 2

And it came to pass in those days, that there went out a decree from Caesar Augustus, that all the world should be taxed.

(And this taxing was first made when Cyrenius was governor of Syria.)

And all went to be taxed, every one into his own city.

And Joseph also went up from Galilee, out of the city of Nazareth, into Judaea, unto the city of David, which is called Bethlehem; (because he was of the house and lineage of David.)

To be taxed with Mary his espoused wife, being great with child.

And so it was, that, while they were there, the days were accomplished that she should be delivered.

And she brought forth her firstborn son, and wrapped him in swaddling clothes, and laid him in a manger; because there was no room for them in the inn.

And there were in the same country shepherds abiding in the field, keeping watch over their flock by night.

And, lo, the angel of the Lord came upon them, and the glory of the Lord shone round about them: and they were sore afraid.

And the angel said unto them, fear not: for, behold, I bring you good tidings of great joy, which shall be to all people.

For unto you is born this day in the city of David a Saviour, which is Christ the Lord.

And this shall be a sign unto you; Ye shall find the babe wrapped in swaddling clothes, and lying in a manger.

And suddenly there was with the angel a multitude of the heavenly host praising God, and saying,

Glory to God in the highest, and on earth peace, good will toward men.

And it came to pass, as the angels were gone away from them into heaven, the shepherds said one to another, Let us now go even unto Bethlehem, and see this thing which has come to pass, which the Lord hath made known unto us.

And they came with haste, and found Mary, and Joseph, and the babe lying in a manger.

And when they had seen it, they made known abroad the saying which was told them concerning this child.

And all they that heard it wondered at those things which were told them by the shepherds.

But Mary kept all these things, and pondered them in her heart.

And the shepherds returned, glorifying and praising God for all the things that they had heard and seen, as it was told unto them.

And when eight days were accomplished for the circumcising of the child, his name was called JESUS, which was so named of the angel before he was conceived in the womb.

After this recitation, Paul told the group he would like to share a little humor with them, since it was a festive occasion. Here is a sample of that humor.

1. Two old guys, longtime friends, were talking one day. One said to the other, "My memory is really goin'. I'm having trouble rememberin' things. Say, was it you or your brother that got killed in the war?"

2. An old guy went to his doctor and had a lot of tests done. The doctor told him to come back the next week. When he got there, the doctor said, "Well, I hate to tell you this, but I've got really bad news and I've got worse news."

   "Doc, that's awful," the man said. "What's the really bad news?"

   Doc answered, "Well, according to all the tests you had done, you only have a week to live."

   "That's awful, Doc," he exclaimed. "What could be worse news?"

   "I should have told you last week," the Doc explained.

3. An old geezer had lived to be 106 years old, and everybody was impressed. At his birthday celebration, reporters and cameramen were there, all hoping to gain some wisdom from him about longevity. "How on earth have you managed to get to be 106 years old?" they asked. "I ain't died yet, that's how" was his answer.

4. An insurance agent pulled up to a new customer's yard and saw a young boy inside the fence with a dog. Being wary of the dog, the man asked the boy, "Does your dog bite?" "No, sir!" was the answer. As the agent started through the gate, the dog growled. "Are you sure your dog won't bite?" he asked the boy. "My dog don't bite," came the answer, so the agent moved on into the yard. When the dog finally turned him loose and he got back out of the gate with his ripped clothes and bleeding leg, he angrily said to the boy, "I thought you said your dog didn't bite!" "This ain't my dog," said the boy.

Paul always has a humorous story to tell to brighten your day and lighten your load. Maybe he'll have a new career as a comedian.

Medicare

When Paul turned 65, he now had Medicare Insurance. He retired from full-time work as an agent covering a Debit and began to sell Medicare Advantage plans, which he could only do between Oct. 15th and Dec. 7th of each year, unless the customer turned 65 at some other time of the year, had moved from one state to the other, or had specific ailments.

He's always careful to find the best coverage for his customers, even if it means switching them to a different company where he will receive less pay.

Chapter Eight
Today

Family

Paul is a very proud father and grandfather.

His daughter, Kim, married Rev. Steven Silvey on Mar. 19, 1994. Their first daughter, Elizabeth McKenna, was born April 10, 1997, and Mary Ellison was born April 13, 1999. Steven is the pastor of Covenant Baptist Church in Anderson.

Daughter Paula married Jerry Garton on Sept. 19, 1992. Their daughter, Amber Elizabeth, was born Dec. 11, 1996, and their son, Jerrod Thomas, was born Oct. 14, 1999.

Paul enjoys supporting his grandchildren in all of their activities.

Today

Paul's inclination toward preaching has taken several avenues. As a lay-preacher, he has preached at several local churches, actually being licensed by the Saluda Baptist Association. He preached several times at the Haven of Rest, a shelter for the homeless. For about six years he was responsible for a service each Wednesday night, except the first in the month, at Home With a Heart, a rehabilitation center near Liberty, SC. He enlisted other speakers for three of the nights each month, taking the fifth Wednesday himself and covering for the other speakers when they couldn't be present.

He has taught Sunday School and is presently a Deacon in his church, as he has been in two previous churches of which he was a member. Each week, he drives his friend Jerry, also an insurance agent, to Woodruff to visit Jerry's elderly wife who is a patient in a Nursing Home there.

He has a phenomenal memory for names, probably because of his genuine love for people. He knows just about everyone in town, and he's always interested in what others have to say. He has a "Google map" of Anderson's city streets in his head, but he can get lost when traveling out-of-state. He loves a good joke, a good Western, and good food.

"Salt of the earth," a genuinely good guy. Should be wearing a white hat, wears white hair instead.

And, at age 75, he's still working as an Insurance Agent.

Life/Death

Recently his life-long friend, Preston Vickery, died. Paul was sitting at the foot of his bed as he breathed his last. Preston was a Christian, knew he was headed to heaven, and had stated he wasn't afraid to die. God had given him the grace to face this last trial, so he peacefully breathed his last breath and said goodbye to earth. The loving-care his wife and son gave him during his last days was heart-warming and an inspiration to Paul.

He thought again about seeing people killed when he worked as a policeman, people who had not expected to die that day, who probably weren't spiritually prepared and so could not be peacefully looking forward to heaven as their destination. One second they were alive, the next they were just as dead as one who had been dead a thousand years. He thought about the Scripture that says life is but a vapor—we can't hold it and make it stay.

The most important thing we can do in life is to prepare for the life after death.

Only in knowing Jesus Christ as Savior can one face death in peace and anticipation of life in a better world. Only in knowing Jesus Christ as Savior can one face life here on earth in peace, no matter what the day-to-day struggles may be. Each day is a gift from God, to be enjoyed in fellowship with Him.

With that in mind, Paul moves on to tomorrow and whatever good things God has planned.

To be continued…

Endnotes

[1] Howard Woody, *South Carolina Postcards Volume lX Anderson County* (Charleston SC, Chicago IL, Portsmouth NH, San Francisco CA: Arcadia Publishing, 2003) Introduction.

[2] Ibid.

[3] Ibid.

[4] Ibid.

[5] Ibid, 57.

[6] Ibid, 58.

[7] Ibid, 63.

[8] Ibid, 62.

[9] Ibid, 34.

[10] Ibid, 20.

[11] Ibid, 20.

[12] Ibid, 56.

Other Books by Helen Jordan Davis

The Joshua Principles: How to Possess Your Promised Land

The Nehemiah Principles: Rebuild Your Wall of Protection

The Covenant Principles: What It Means To Be in Covenant with God

The Covenant Principles 2nd Edition: What It Means To Be in Covenant with God

The Genesis Principles: Old Testament Treasures Vol. One

The Christmas Principles: Why Christians MUST Celebrate Christmas

The Christmas Principles 2nd Edition: Why Christians MUST Celebrate Christmas

O-The Story of Oliver and Nadjy

Mickey-Life and Times So Far

Watchman! Have You Been Sleeping?

He Makes All Things Beautiful in His Time

CPSIA information can be obtained at www.ICGtesting.com
Printed in the USA
LVOW11s0219081015

457296LV00001B/1/P